MW00975351

TEA WITH MY CHAOS!

A riotous romp and odyssey of life in a set of Islands
in the West Indies, with a healthy slice of hyperbole

Larry Larking

Published by Tea Cozy Publishing, September 2021
ISBN: 9781916201002

Typeset: Greg Salisbury
Book Cover Design: Judith Mazari

DISCLAIMER: This book is a work of fiction, based on
a true story of the author's life. Names, characters, places or
incidents are either the product of the author's imagination or
are used fictiously. Any resemblance to actual persons, living
or dead, events, or locales is entirely coincidental. Readers of
this publication agree that neither Larry Larking (pen name)
nor his publisher will be held responsible or liable for damages
that may be alleged or resulting directly or indirectly from the
reading of this publication.

"We are but what our dreams are made on,
and our little life rounded in sleep".
William Shakespeare: The Tempest

"To the millions, perhaps on a morning commuter train, who dream of a break from the everyday routine. Just do it. You only live once. Worse things can happen! Reggy Perrin did; metaphorically casting off his clothes on the shoreline and swimming off to new adventures; leaving his boring job behind and all that went with it."

Acknowledgement

To Julie Salisbury, whose inspiring encouragement made this story possible. Also tremendous fun to work with.

Contents

Copywrite II
Dedication V
Acknowledgement VII

Chap 1: A Germ of an Idea 1
Chap 2: A Cast Off or Away? 7
Chap 3: A Sojourn in Nassau 15
Chap 4: And So To Turks 23
Chap 5: Settling In And Setting up 31
Chap 6: Trooping The Brownies And Bring on The Alka Seltzer ... 37
Chap 7: What's It All About, Alfie? 47
Chap 8: Hurricanes Hardly Ever Happen 55
Chap 9: Pan Am And Some Discarded Wrecks 63
Chap 10: Where The Sun Never Sets 71
Chap 11: Our Revolutionary Registrar 77
Chap 12: Specimens And Legal Bovver 83
Chap 13: Of Fireworks And Commissions 89
Chap 14: Beachcoming And Bar Repartee 95
Chap 15: Musings At The Airport 105
Chap 16: Salt Cay 111
Chap 17: Goldmining, Wind And Banking 119
Chap 18: Prime Rib Night 127
Chap 19: Itchy Feet And Treading Water 135
Chap 20: Westward Ho 145
Chap 21: Provo, The Huck Finn Isle 155
Chap 22: The Container Has Landed 165
Chap 23: Boating With JoJo 175
Chap 24: Bozo To Dog Baskets 183
Chap 25: Momentous Events 191
Chap 26: A Question of Security, Panama Jack and 007 199

Chap 27: Confy 207
Chap 28: It's a Dogs Life 215
Chap 29: And The World Turned Upside Down 223
Chap 30: Wrexit and Lemon Aid...................................... 229

Epilogue 237
Biography .... ,,, .,,.. 239

Chapter 1

A Germ of an Idea

I remember as if it were only yesterday. Crikey! Come to think of it, that's the start of Treasure Island, where Jim Hawkins commences his tale years later by way of reminiscence. Anyway, I'll stick with it, because there are parallels. A curious turn of events which took him from England on an unexpected journey to the West Indies, in what amounted to a life changer.

It was thirty-five years ago to be precise. As a solicitor, I was fortunate enough to be in Nicmanees, a leading City of London practice. Established over one hundred and fifty years; with a remarkable clientele, ranging from peers of the realm to the pin striped wonders of the City. A bit royal as a colleague once imparted to me. But they were smart. Never over expanding to become one of those impersonal monoliths typical of today. On the ball, independent and well connected. It all somehow added up. I was like a tram, well set on its rails and never seemingly deemed to step out of the ruts.

Funny, isn't it, how things change and without any foresight. It was late one Friday afternoon and I was closing a matter at another solicitor's office, just off Wigmore Street in the West End. The principal never seemed to be there and the work was entrusted to a newly qualified solicitor. A very personable fellow called Toby, who sensibly realized he was a bit out of his depth then and asked for my help, albeit I was on the other side as it were, which I did with alacrity.

The bomb he dropped at the conclusion of our business could have knocked my socks off. " I suppose I told you that I have decided to turn down my career move to the Turks and Caicos Islands, I'm simply not ready for it yet and need to learn more here". Only the previous Sunday there had been an article in one of the leading journals (Sunday Times, as I recall) by Hal Geezerberger, a famous American tax planning lawyer, extolling the virtues of the Turks and Caicos Islands as an exotic offshore potential as a finance centre and for tourist related development and what's more a colony of the U.K.to boot!

Up until that point most people, yours truly included, had never heard of the place; unless you happened to be a diving nut or a philatelist with a penchant for unusual stamps. Coincidence? All that night I couldn't stop thinking about it, with a sense of adventure; perhaps rare for one in the legal fraternity in those days . It was a germ of an idea from which an acorn was sown with an oak tree as the result. Or perhaps more pertinently, a trickle, a stream, a river and four and a half thousand miles later a voyage across an ocean.

But there were preliminaries which had to be dealt with. In any case I had to learn more. Curiously enough my wife, who loved travel, was gung ho on the idea. Without that endorsement, you go nowhere fast. Ruminating upon the issue in our small Westminster flat that evening there was much to consider. Being from London, even if there was mileage in this seeming lunacy which I hadn't even explored yet, leaving would be a wrench up to a point and, something along the lines of

Dr. Johnson's quotation, "when a man is tired of London, he is tired of life" does tend to cross the bows of your mind. Albeit that I wouldn't miss my mandatory two common colds a year, the damp and the cold in winter.

Bottom line and deep down, notwithstanding the life style and interesting people and situations, I really was looking for a change. The prospect ahead of years of answering hundreds of pre-contract multi preliminary enquires, reading local authority search results and tedious documents, heralded about as much potential satisfaction as watching a cricket test match for days on end or looking at paint dry. In short, it had become a bit like working in a sausage factory.

So I pursued the line of enquiry and ended up contacting the principal, Orlando Besbequick, who turned out to be a well established lawyer/accountant in Nassau in the Bahamas. He was a local who had also at one time held very senior positions in the Central Bank there. He had a law practice and investment company and was eager to set up in the Turks and Caicos Islands, a jurisdiction being flavour of the month as it were right then, as an emerging offshore centre. The idea was to meet his London agent, who had the use of an office in Trafalgar Square, to see what the position entailed and if that turned out alright to come out to Nassau for further discussions.

So at the appointed time I duly toddled down to Trafalgar Square to further the story. There is something about Trafalgar Square that is so quintessentially patriotic, British, embodiment of spirit call it what you will. The atmosphere overwhelms. I always remember the film A Town Like Alice (Nevil Shute) when Peter Finch, in love with Virginia McKenna (a pin up of mine), travels from Australia to seek her out via her solicitor's office, which happens to be in where else, Trafalgar Square. Only to find she had gone in the opposite direction to a derelict cattle station called Alice to find him. Anyway, you get the drift.

If you have never been in those buildings before it is something of an experience. Most have been in the National Gallery; in fact I attended a reunion of my London law firm there just a few years ago. The building for the interview consisted of a vast cavernous hallway. Very dark with just dim lights. High ceilings and overall conveying a sense of foreboding. It hadn't seen a lick of paint in a century at least.

The lift, it could have been Otis's prototype, was huge. With savage concertina fashioned gates that crashed across as you entered, simply wanting to do you injury. The slow deep whirring of the machinery as it carried you slowly up to what must have been the top floor. You almost felt you were on your way to meet your maker. It must have taken ages and was certainly on the top floor. Upon approaching the large old door I wondered what awaited the other side. Perhaps a sinister Blofeld type, out of the Bond movies, seated in a black executive chair and stroking a fluffy white cat in his lap.

Upon knocking and entering the room I was surprised to meet a genial man by the name of Freddy Flotsam. He could have been a character out of Pickwick Papers. Half moon brass spectacles perched midway down his nose. Certainly rotund in stature, sporting a tweed jacket and a v-necked woolen sweater. Quite a pleasant contrast given the portender to my entry; I had half been expecting the grim reaper himself. He sat behind a large desk on one of those enormous revolving chairs which he clearly had no control over. Hands crossed with contemplative ease over his ample abdomen. His antics reminded me slightly of Inspector Clousseau and his disastrous encounters with minor objects. For example the letter opener flew out of his hand when he gesticulated and hit a stern looking nineteenth century bearded gentleman portrayed in an oil painting on the wall.

Anyway most importantly he was pleasant and did his best to answer my questions and thought a visit to Nassau a better bet in order to get fuller answers, which was what his principal wanted anyway. Again the room was itself dark but was hit with blazing light from an ample window. It was so high up I was seemingly looking at Nelson himself and could have sworn he was winking at me out of his good eye.

The end of the interview took a different turn. He was hoping his principal would see the merit of investing in some business ventures he was contemplating and he wanted to run them by me. One of them comprised of setting up cut price motor insurance shops not far from the major motorways in the UK. Perhaps catering for those who ordinarily had difficulties in getting cover. As politely as I could I indicated that in my view this wasn't the hottest idea since the invention of sliced bread. He took it in good humour and simply muttered "just a thought", "just a thought".

I found myself in Nassau about a month later. It was my first visit to this part of the world. It conveyed a somewhat dumpy run down impression but obviously a great tourist attraction with the glaring beaches, azure sea, palm trees and its multi catering resorts. Undoubtedly it had character and Bay Street was its main and famous thoroughfare. This was my exploratory visit and to see if a deal as it were was on the cards.

One thing you learn to appreciate when you are visiting other parts of the world is that customs and protocol often follow a very different pattern to what is your expected norm. The lawyer I was dealing with was extremely personable and clearly able. But sometimes I found in negotiations that when perhaps the discussions or terms were not going quite the way that was desired, the whole subject matter was thrown up in the air, so that you would have to start all over again. Rather like wrecking a partly completed jigsaw puzzle just because some pieces didn't fit. There was no unpleasantness about it; it was just a way of doing business. Anyway an agreement was reached, contemplating that Nassau would be my base and that the Turks and Caicos Islands venture would be assessed down the road as it were. It simply remained to tie up our affairs in London and commence in Nassau six months later.

Chapter 2

A Cast Off or Away?

Was it Elizabeth Gaskell who said "I'll not listen to reason, because it always means having to listen to what someone else has to say"? That was pretty much the impression I got as to the opinion held of me when I imparted news of my intended venture to family and colleagues. Probably also thought that a much needed trip to the funny farm was called for, although they were too polite to say as much.

Without trying to sound hubristic, there is a sort of parochial resentment which people in the UK not infrequently feel when you come out with something that is wholly out of the norm. As if how could you possibly want to leave the U.K. Life after all stopped at Luton Airport (Okay I'm making that up, but you get my general tenor).

Actually there was a somewhat unnerving twist to all this. It came shortly after my return from Nassau. Depending upon where you are in London, it simply oozes with atmosphere. My flat in Westminster, in fact close to Vincent Square, even had a view of the Victoria Tower and Big Ben over the roof tops. Commuting each day was a trip down history lane. Why is it that when you make a commitment in life, some little gremlin seemingly emerges from the heavens and comes to sit on your shoulder and illustrates with fervent passion the attractiveness of what you are giving up. Much like Scrooge's ghosts (although in reverse and not sinister).

My commute each day was unusual by any standards. First there was the option of walking down Horseferry Road to Lambeth Bridge or alternatively cutting through the great Georgian houses around Lord North Street and the many famous personages they must have housed. Either way you were eventually confronted with the Thames and more or less emerged west of the Victoria Tower and the consequent walk past the Houses of Parliament (wishing Rick the Lionheart and Olly Cromwell a pleasant morning as I did so) until I reached Big Ben. When, if I was lucky and on the hour, it would sound forth its rich, inimitable, deep resonant peels (much better than the Arthur J. Rank's gong in so many British films). The only hiccup to this daily ramble being if it rained. Then a quick if hazardous crossing of the road at Westminster Bridge and like a mole scurrying deep into the bowels of Westminster Station for the fifteen minute ride to Temple Station and to my office not far from there.

One evening (it must have been a few days after my return from Nassau) I chose to walk along the embankment instead of taking the train segment of my journey. It was beginning to darken and as I passed Scott's Discovery which took him to the South Pole, the lights began to twinkle across the river along with the towering Victorian lamp posts I was passing under. A breeze ran through the trees somewhat eerily and the river traffic was still quite plentiful. You could also see the succession of bridges in the distance. The Thames is a remarkable river and it was easy to see why Manet wanted to paint it at dusk. Writers were drawn to it as well. Dickens in Great Expectations, Conan

Doyle in the Sign of Four and that great testimony to the river and the antics it suffers, J.K. Jerome's Three Men In A Boat; the latter undoubtedly being my proclivity, given my aptitude for mishaps.

One of my last assignments before embarking on my West Indies venture consisted of evaluating a large country estate. This was not uncommon with the type of practice I was in and actually often turned out to be a not unpleasant escapade in the country.

Unless you are dealing with Chatsworth House , Castle Howard or Highclear Castle (Downton Abbey), it may be surprising to learn that many stately homes, as they are called, lie off the beaten track and, unless equipped with a good map, can be exceedingly hard to find. So it was the case here. Talbot Hall lay some twenty-five miles south west of Norwich having achieved a well earned obscurity for anyone trying to find it. Luckily I had an old map book for the UK; it was a family heirloom which went into exorbitant detail, showing almost every hamlet, tracks even in the country and I would never have reached my quarry without it. Even so, and true to form, I managed to get lost.

At long last, having meandered seemingly forever down a stone walled country lane, the walls gave way to ornamental railings of a fence, behind which lay cultivated wooded parkland, which seemed to go on for at least a couple of a miles. I took this to be the halfway point because to my left I came upon a magnificent stoned gateway with enormous iron gates. It had an emblem at its pinnacle depicting something I couldn't make out (perhaps a gargoyle!). Certainly no Avon lady or double glazing salesman were going to strike gold here. There was a box with a button at the side. Upon pressing and after a few minutes a polite and genial voice enquired who I was and upon answering the great gates slowly parted and I was in. It seemed to take an age to get to the Hall. Alright, I know, stop exaggerating.

Upon reaching the main entrance along a graveled drive I was met by the current owner, Hon. Hugo Templeton-Hughes. If ever there was the perfect personification of the English gentleman he was it to a tee. Friendly as well, without any tinge of condescension that can sometimes accompany the ennobled classes. At least six foot two in height, supremely fit and cultivated to a fault. He had actually been a Grenadier Guards officer and one could easily see him doing the honours at Trooping the Colour. He had a sense of purpose to him and strength of character, fully in keeping with his whole DNA. He lived at the hall with his wife, who was charming, and as far as I can tell there were only about two other helpers in the running of the whole enterprise.

My brief was to undertake an evaluation of the title of the entire estate, which included several tenancies, some of them agricultural. I delighted in this sort of undertaking. It involved going through in some instances ancient deeds (still with the seals in their metal boxes) and to some extent it was an historical quasi sleuthing exercise to see how it all fitted together. Nowadays, with land registries, I imagine this sort of thing to be a rarity and title work has probably become humdrum conveyor belt business. The estate merited being inspected, which turned out to be a pleasant jaunt in an electric golf cart; it had a beautiful lake and picturesque woodland, apart from the arable land.

That night proved interesting. My hosts, due to the smallness of their retinue to run the place, had their meals in the kitchen. I say kitchen, but it was more the size of an ordinary house. The culinary side was impeccable. My host's ancestor, who had commissioned the Hall, was in fact the founder of the temperance movement. Thankfully abstinence hadn't filtered down to the current incumbent of the Hall, and we polished off at least a couple bottles of fine claret plus numerous glasses of port.

I had earlier been given a truncated tour of the Hall, since it was vast. It also had two extensive wings (which I will come to in a jiff). My main memory was of the main hall itself. It could have been one of the main galleries at the Natural History Museum for sheer size and grandeur. It was seemingly stacked as far as the eye could see with suits of armor, military uniforms, banners, flags and accoutrements of war. I don't think I have ever seen such an array of sinister hardware designed to dispatch people off the mortal coil.

Bedtime was something else altogether. I was to be put in the West Wing. Getting there seemed like a trek. Up some old wide staircase which gave way to a hallway that seemed to go on to infinity. A vast dimly lit high ceilinged passageway which about half way along lead to my room for the night. Again high ceilings (the theme of this place), dark and cavernous (visitations of Trafalgar Square were coming back to haunt me). In fact everything made you feel like a midget in proportion to the surroundings; although I was close to six feet tall myself . The bath was about eight feet long, with taps that looked like they had been lifted from the Trevi Fountain. As I later found out when you sat in it you couldn't see over the rim. This stuff had Bates Motel written all over it. The best was yet to come.

I always find it difficult sleeping away from home, at least in strange surroundings and I drifted off into a truncated sort of sleep as it must have been just passed midnight. Suddenly I was awoken by screaming sirens which echoed throughout the Hall. Scrambling for my watch I saw it was just gone two in the morning. What the heck to do. My natural inclination was to beat a retreat under the bed. After about ten minutes it all ceased, although I did not relish opening the huge door. The rest of the night was uneventful, but it ranks number one in my all time record of spooky experiences.

Next morning at breakfast Hugo wondered how I hadn't heard the alarm. He had gone out armed to see what may have been a foot. Very much as you would expect of him. Anyway nothing was amiss. In response to the question I took a gulp of tea and said " goodness no, I didn't hear a thing-slept like a log". Ann, his wife gave me a kindly and knowing smile. Lying was never my forte.

The rest of the visit went swimmingly. But when I got home I couldn't help but ponder, that I would probably never come across this rich pageant of experience again, with this new venture I was contemplating. How wrong I was to be!

I won't bore you with the last peregrinations leading to my departure. Only to say that we were able to let our flat. Oddly enough it was to an M.P. Sir Guisholme de Paine, one of Margaret Thatcher's ministers (one of her so called whets, as it turned out). Curiously enough, my now erstwhile firm acted for him. The attraction of the place being that it was close for the division bell in the House. Have you noticed how many knights and lords there are nowadays in Parliament? The clanking of armor in the House must be positively deafening!

I will never forget his inspection of the place. A tall gaunt man sporting one of those prosperous looking dark blue coats with a black velvet collar; usually bestowed upon people of importance. Giving the place no more than a cursory glance and swirling with an air of no time to waste, he simply said "it will suit my purposes". Evidently a man used to being treated with deference and I don't even recall him looking at us. Somehow I felt like the visitor. The details were left to his pleasant diminutive aide, a nice blue stockinged young lady (probably straight out of Roedean and Burkes Peerage) to conclude, whilst he wafted off to more important engagements.

A further episode occurs to me in that I might not have embarked on my venture at all. On one of my last assignments a senior member of the firm, who happened to be an avid pilot, wanted to fly a leading barrister of Kings Bench Walk and myself to a meeting in Norfolk (somehow it was always Norfolk). We gathered at his aircraft at a remote aerodrome south of London, if I remember correctly. Trouble was there was fog everywhere, even at our destination in Norfolk. Having an instrument rating he was "keen to have a go and chance it" to use his words. The barrister, who resembled something along the lines of Rumpole of the Bailey, rapidly turned bilious at this pronouncement and said he couldn't face it. So thankfully we were off the hook, much to the chagrin of our disappointed Biggles.

Farewells were duly made and 1st January 1984 found us on a BA flight bound for Nassau and whatever else that held in store.

Chapter 3

A Sojourn in Nassau

Nothing happens fast in Nassau and that was before you even disembarked from the plane. There was a queue of about four planes waiting to disgorge their passengers. But everyone was given drinks whilst waiting and the captain did a public relations tour down the isles. A tall, slim silvery headed gent with a manicured moustache and positively wreaking of experience. In fact he would have been a better bet for an ad in those days for B.A. than the Mike Sammes singers with their "up up and away". This was the type of guy who was always going to get you down in one piece. The ladies were purring.

Anyway off we hopped eventually and joined the ponderous line at Immigration. Where after an eternity we were confronted by a very large uniformed gentleman with various badges on his apparel. I couldn't help noticing an enormous gold ring on his finger with what must have been a sapphire mounted of equal proportions. Maybe he was an eccentric millionaire who liked to do this job as a pastime. He had multiple gold chains around his neck and could have done a decent pass off as "Mr. T." After studiously flicking through our passports he stamped them heavily with something that resembled and sounded like a power compressor. He smiled , revealing the largest and whitest set of teeth I had ever seen; you almost needed sunglasses to cope with the glare. "Welcome to the Bahamas" he said.

Strangely customs was almost deserted and emerging from the airport we were cheerily met by Orlando, who checked us into a hotel just on Bay Street after about a half hours drive. Any notions of sleeping off jet lag were out of the question. Tonight was Junkanoo night. If you haven't seen this you are missing something. It is an all night carnival and ranks only after Rio and Trinidad in size. It happens on Boxing day with a repeat on the ensuing New Year's Day every year and all year is taken preparing the floats and costumes. It's a spectacular fanfare with a reverberative beat that goes on perpetually. In short a good time had by all, with drink and food a plenty.

I am going to keep my recollections of the Nassau experience to a series of small vignettes, because for practical reasons it did not last that long; in fact about three months in total. The working conditions and people were nice. The office being in Bay Street, although old, had character. It had to be kept in mind that I had embarked on a career move and the working future was of paramount importance; especially in terms of longevity. To work you were dependent upon having a work permit as a non-Bahamian; permanent residence being almost unheard of, and the reissuance of these work permits fell into that category of the indeterminate vicissitudes of working life there.

Whilst Orlando had me happily working behind the scenes in his law practice, the hard fact of the matter was , that as a non-Bahamian, I could never be admitted to practice law there. Sir Linden Pindling, the Prime Minister, had embarked on a programme of Bahamianisation; which meant encouraging all good positions of employment to be filled with Bahamians, which is entirely understandable and constituted the philosophy of their immigration policy. By contrast, I could be admitted to practice law in the Turks and Caicos Islands and the attainment of permanent residence (as I will allude to later) was a much easier process.

Also, unbeknown to me when I arrived, a commission of enquiry had just been set up to examine allegations regarding the use of certain islands in the Bahamian chain for refuelling stops for drug runners from South America; sending their illicit inbound cargo to America. Allegedly it had ramifications for certain high up personages and although, if memory serves correctly, nothing was actually proved which could substantiate further action, it nevertheless had an unsettling effect as to the desirability of the place for doing business. However that said, Nassau was in fact one of the major centres in the world for the euro-dollar market. Just about every known bank had a presence there.

Bay Street was a curious place with its straw market, vendors, shops and tourist attractions. The cruise ships used to tie up at the port and thousands of their passengers spilling onto the street was the resulting chaos. The colonial style government buildings lay down the street, where the world famous Royal Bahamian Police Band would give renditions and perform, with incredible precision. They were in fact world class entertainment. They had an incredible repertoire and people would be dancing to their music. They had resplendent uniforms with white pith royal marine style helmets. I well remember the leading drum major, an enormous man with a leopard skin over his tunic, throwing the huge ornamental baton seemingly thirty feet into the air and catching it without even looking, eyes fixed ahead of him as he marched.

On the all essential watering hole side of things and for lunchtime sustenance, the professional community had The Green Shutters Pub just off Bay Street (sadly now a figment of past gone days), where the cask ale beer flowed more than it probably should have done. And the food! Steak and kidney/ shepherds pie, bangers and mash and fish and chips, challenging the best of what any culinary establishment back in England could come up with (Okay, a bit of hyperbole, but it was good). Trouble was working afterwards.

Accommodation wise? Well, quite frankly we were spoilt. Across from Nassau, over a surrealistically high arching bridge, lies the small Paradise Island .I think it was bought by the Swedish magnate who was the founder of Electrolux back in the 1950's. At the East end of the Island he sought to recreate the gardens at Versailles and by importing the requisite means to do so he succeeded in creating what you might term a micro version of the same. It was also integrated with a luxurious hotel called Ocean Club; the setting for the latest Bond 'Casino Royale' film just a few years back.

At the other end of the Island an internment camp called Club Med had set up. Whilst in the centre facing what was the pristine Cabbage Beach, three magnificent hotels stood there (I think at the time Hollywood mogul Merv Griffin had an interest in the Island). In crude tourist terms that was the piece de resistance. There were the three linked hotels with a large casino and entertainment theatre. I remember it as 'Britannia Towers'. It was our access to Vegas. The shows were stupendous and many a hard working person in Nassau went there to let off steam and down more than a few lethal libations at the weekends.

Where did my home fit into this? Well just between this hotel complex and Ocean Club an affluent German developer called Fritz Brickymeier had built a series of new duplexes just adjacent to Cabbage Beach. It was within a walled compound with pool. In style it looked like something you would see in Marrakesh. His wife, Frau Brickymeier was very nice, an ample lady who resembled something off a Pauli Girl beer bottle label, only much bigger.

I well remember walking into the apartment the day before we moved in. There was the loud noise of a transistor radio coming from one of the internal bathrooms. It was the tiler. I called out to him to see if all was well. It was pitch black as there was no electricity yet. He stuck his head out from the entrance way saying "you bet man". A cheery fellow, but he was wearing sunglasses! I could only conclude that he had a mental picture of what to do. Actually the end product was fine surprisingly. The apartment was very spacious and nicely laid out, with a pond and garden at the rear.

Bars on your windows were a necessity, because crime even in those days was of pressing concern. In fact Paradise Island had its own security detachment. Not that we encountered any problems. A local friend at work, Herbie, invited us to a basketball game one night in a community more in the centre of the Island. Where you would not expect to find tourists or expats. Although there was some trepidation, as being so obviously from outside, and crime was a reality in Nassau, it was as if the people there sensed that and went out of their way to be hospitable. It was touching. The game was exciting and we came back having relished the experience having had a good time.

The shows at Britannia Towers were an inevitable attraction and it was only a short well lit walk away. I remember upon one occasion waiting for my wife in one of the foyers. She had gone off to the washroom. Suddenly I was approached by a truly exotic , dark and well dressed lady who enquired "Have you the time hon?". Beaming back stupidly I looked at my watch and said "Yes of course, 8-30pm". Whereupon she rolled her eyes to heaven, shrugged her shoulders and stomped off irritably so it seemed. My wife came back and asked if I had been bored waiting to which I responded "not in the least ".

Later, when I recounted the event to a local friend, he laughed and indicated in no uncertain terms that "have you the time" meant something else altogether. Alright, I'm from London and not especially naive, but my usual haunts there were scarcely Shepherds Market, Soho or the other more insalubrious areas of London.

The expat community was unusual. Being one you inevitably become embroiled in one of their social groups at some stage. So it was through my wife. On one occasion we were invited to a splendorous residence in Nassau, which could easily cater to scores of people for a cocktail party. This was like a tropical stately home, you almost expected to find footmen. The ladies invariably tend to the organizing of these functions and as it turned out the lady who owned this residence had a husband who was an inventor. I can't remember his name but his claim to fame was inventing a simple but innovative type of plastic swivel top. It had achieved massive application commercially and hence their wealth and sumptuous lifestyle. He was decidedly a bit cocooned within himself in a somewhat eccentric manner and looked markedly professorial with an uncontrollable mop of hair. This guy had made a packet and I was to personally sample his product a week or so later during a weekend visit to Miami.

We were in International House of Pancakes for lunch, a popular restaurant and quite noisy. I was wanting to season my beef roll with some mustard. And much to my surprise and delight the very plastic bottle whose creator I had met stood in front of me, the swivel neck encrusted in mustard. I swiveled the swivel so to speak and squeezed as hard as I could, but nothing came out. Took a deep breath and gave an almighty squeeze. BANG, an explosion, you somehow immediately knew what had happened and I felt spatters of gooey substance spray all over me. The restaurant went deadly quiet. I was covered in the stuff and my wife was giggling. All that remained was for me to be lead outside by the hand like a bewildered chimpanzee. That afternoon, after clean up, I researched purchasing a box of exploding cigars to dispatch to my inventor acquaintance (an absolute lie of course, but I felt like it).

It brought to mind an episode in one of my favourite films, 'Kind Hearts and Coronets'. Where Dennis Price, in his murderous bid to secure an aristocratic title he was wrongly deprived of, dispatches one of his victims (a verbose and garrulous general ahead of him in the succession) by sending him a jar of explosive mustard to him at his club. He then recounts his dispassionate views on the subject with a delightful line "revenge, as the Italians so eloquently put it, is the dish which people of taste best prefer served cold." Absolutely delicious and I am day dreaming again.

Back in Nassau, Orlando was plainly more keen to centre operations there, whilst I favoured giving Turks and Caicos a try. My wife and I (sounds regal) had carried out a lot of research on the place a few weeks earlier and although unusual by any standards, there was a curious attraction to it. We therefore amicably agreed to go our separate ways and so the real fun began.

Chapter 4

And So To Turks

At Miami Airport there came the tannoy announcement "Cayman Airways Flight to Grand Turkey will depart from Gate 39 at 2-35 p.m." It was the only commercial flight to the Islands in those days; Air Florida having just gone bust and Grand Turk was its stopover en route back to Cayman. Clearly we were not a well known destination yet. Nowadays Providenciales is the main airport with virtually all the main airlines flying directly there on a daily basis. Given the vicissitudes of air travel then we were thankful for that; even if it was just two days a week.

Even more interesting was the flight itself. There were just five passengers on board including ourselves. And yet this was a 727 jet; financial viability obviously didn't figure into the equation. The flight down there takes about one and a half hours and you fly over the entire chain of the Bahamian Family Islands; some 575 miles south. It is an unforgettable sight looking down with these brilliant islands encircled in pure white beaches and green scrub bush interiors in an endless sparkling azure blue sea.

I found myself hypnotized, wondering what on earth went

on down there. Occasionally you would make out mankind's contribution in the form of a track leading to some remote cluster of dwellings usually from a rough line of an airstrip hewn out in the middle of nowhere. There were also boats moored far below and some making a wake as they cruised between the islands.

As the plane circled on reaching our destination I caught a brief glimpse of what seemed like a small island; in fact it is some eight miles long and about half a mile wide, with a population mustering some 2500 people then, with what appeared like some creeks and a dull interior shallow lake. My concern was, upon looking at the airstrip, it just seemed too short. Down we came, bit by bit, suddenly a tree and a fence flew passed the window and then bang, bang, bang as each wheel hit the tarmac with a resounding thud. The screeching application of brakes or deflected thrust whatever it is that stops the contraption and meanwhile us praying that we don't run out of airstrip. And then it stopped, turned slowly, and we indeed realized that we had used up the entire runway.

Unclasping our hands to the Almighty we took in from out the window our first impressions. Derelict didn't do it justice. A discarded bus, a cannibalized light aircraft, scavenging dogs and a braying donkey were our first introduction. An aircraft hangar resembling one of those wartime nissan huts went passed as we trundled to a stop, about two hundred yards from the airport terminal, which looked something like a Foreign Legion outpost from Beau Geste.

What you have to appreciate is the fact that our arrival was simply the highlight of the week to the residents and they had turned out in full. As evidenced by their numbers, faces pressing against the perimeter fencing of the airport terminal. Full of anticipation and clinging to the fencing like internees of a mental institution with wild anticipation at the arrival of visitors.

A truly pleasant, jovial large lady dealt with the immigration formalities and quickly let us through. Why is it immigration officials often are so large. Perhaps because it is a somewhat sedentary occupation with little else to do for much of the time. I did notice a discarded number of what looked like chicken bones in foil at the side of the desk. Anyway her good humour was infectious, as was needed when it came collecting our luggage. This was seemingly discharged though a hole in the wall, along with an assortment of car parts, pipes, items ordered from Miami and so forth.

One case was missing and when mentioning it to an official, he sprinted back out to the plane or its dispatcher and cheerily appeared with it about five minutes later. Our customs form, along with immigration, had been completed on the plane and upon the official asking any "any fruit or veggies?" I was tempted to say "sure I'll take a dozen bananas and some cauliflowers", but of course I didn't. We were carelessly ushered through and out of the building without further ado.

First impressions of Grand Turk? Wow! Generally, it was like being on H.G. Well's "Time Machine" and , instead of being catapulted forward, being yanked back one hundred and fifty years. Time truly had stood still here. Of course there were cars; although many looking as if they were on their last legs. The buildings were overall faded and much discarded. But when you drove from the airport downtown to Front Street, about a mile away, the picture changed . This was Cockburn Town and where it (whatever it was) all happened so to speak, being the capital of Grand Turk.

There is some essential geography that well merits being mapped out here. You emerge onto the seafront at what was the Kittina Hotel in those days and from there passed a series of very old dwellings, some wooden and some stone, with neatly fenced gardens down to what was the Salt Raker Inn; going back at least one hundred and fifty years. Owned and ran by Hank Scoopo (a retired Hollywood publicist) and his elegant English wife, Elise. Walking is essential and delightful here. The sea lapping to your left with casaurena trees, their evergreen needles making eerie noises as the breeze whisks through them. A further one hundred yards down the one way road you find the seemingly makeshift Papillon Restaurant apparently projecting right out to the sea. Run by a delightfully eccentric Frenchman, Pierre Langoutse and his two common law wives.

A little thereafter on the right comes the famous "Turks Head Inn". A renowned watering hole and centre of great sagacial debate by its local and well known clientele (to be alluded to further). Its proprietor was an amiable American, Bud Allyoucan, the soul of hospitality. It was rumoured (no shortage of those in Grand Turk) that he was a remittance man from a wealthy family who simply chose to chill out in Grand Turk. All the characters warrant elaboration but I will make brief references just now, concentrating on the layout of the place.

From the Turks Head Inn for about two hundred yards there follows a delightful avenue of trees with spectacular flowering almost precluding sunlight. On either side they mask old houses, set well back. High white walls lined the avenue. To the left the old residence of the Discardi Brothers (wealthy, somewhat reclusive Jewish Jamaicans who ran an importing business). Beyond them a grey wooden tall house, forever shuttered, and occupied by a tall elderly and distinguished local lady, Ms. Princepen, who very rarely ventured forth, but upon doing so was always turned out in resplendent fashion in her Sunday best, a reminder of the thirties.

On some further and opposite lived Ray Bridenorth, a civil engineer working for government, but formerly managing director of a large UK engineering firm in the Midlands; this was a sinecure for him. And to complete the avenue at the very end, The Ramparts, a maze of rooms and commercial space, owned and run by Alfie Tryon and his wife Esmeralda. He had come after the Second World War, in fact sometime in the fifties, from Jamaica to help the Administrator (then Governor) in an accounting/administrative capacity.

Then Front Street opened up with purely the sea and the old seawall on the west side. Immediately on the right was the large Cable & Wireless complex (the long serving communications company for the Islands). This in architectural terms was the only carbuncle on the landscape; spoiler if you will. It was typical of that 1950's bland minimalistic style, somewhat reminiscent of Chiswick underground station in London, I thought. With a tower displaying an impersonal dotted circle clock.

But after that a mixture of ochre coloured government buildings , churches, a few shops, Government itself, Victorian Library and lodge, all old and historic, extending for about a quarter of a mile in a gentle curve. They positively oozed character. Culminating with an ancient dock at the end, where Haitian and Dominican sloops would offload their cargoes of fruit and vegetables from Hispaniola. This was pure picture postcard stuff; with donkeys and the odd cow ambling along the thoroughfare. Take the occasional car or truck out of it and you were transported back to the 1860's.

Parallel to Front Street and to the East lay Pond Street and immediately adjacent to that the salt Salinas, long since disused with an odor redolent of staleness and brackish water which is what it was. For many years salt was the backbone to the economy to the Islands. Originally in the late 17th century Bermudians had come to rake salt, hence the salinas. It was so valuable as a preservative that at one time it was termed "white gold". The industry had proven so successful that sometime in the 1850's there had been counted one hundred horse drawn carriages at the Governor's residence, Waterloo, on the south west side of the Island.

However the irrefutable and disgraceful fact remains that the success of this industry was predicated, for many years up until the 1830's, upon slave labour and the terrible deprivations suffered by the ancestors of the current Islander population. Salt subsequently declined as a commercial proposition here and nowadays it is still carried on in Great Inagua.; the Bahamian island some one hundred miles to the West where the famous Morton company has a presence. It had continued on in our own Salt Cay until the early 1960's ; a wonderful little island which can be seen just a few miles to the south east of Grand Turk and which features later in this missive.

There is a hinterland to Grand Turk with various communities. To the north lies North Creek, a large natural inlet popular with boating traffic and a smaller one to the south, east of the airport . High on the north east side the road rises to about one hundred feet and continues along what is called the Ridge, which eventually culminates in a lighthouse built in 1852 to protect shipping (ship wrecking I later found out, was somewhat of a cottage industry in the Islands at one time). Off the ridge either side of the road are various homes with splendid views of the ocean.

Apart from the lay out of the place, a little potted history doesn't go amiss either. The Spanish at one time possessed the Islands, then the French and Nelson suffered one of his rare defeats here in trying to take Grand Turk from the French. However the Islands firmly became British, administered via The Bahamas and then Jamaica. When Jamaica became independent in 1962 the Islands remained with the U.K.. John Glenn was debriefed here (interrogation wise I mean) after his famous space orbital mission in 1962. A replica of his space capsule sits outside Grand Turk Airport today.

For many years the mainstay of the economy here had been dependent upon the existence of two U.S. tracking stations; one at the southern tip and the other by the lighthouse at the northern most point run by the Navy, known as North and South Bases. Typically with the U.S. service regime in those days they were excellently equipped and even had cinemas, restaurants and generally were a source of uplift for the Islands. Their closure in the early eighties came as a blow to the economy; simply with satellites the work needed was more economically dealt with Stateside. As a consequence, the UK encouraged the development of offshore/ tax haven work as a boost, to plug the hole left in the economy, and in those days helped effect legislation to achieve that goal. Hence the presence now of yours truly.

I cannot end this mapping and story aspect without extolling Grand Turk's greatest claim to fame. To those in the know, it is an established fact that this was where Columbus made his first landing in the New World in 1492. No kidding, and the historical data bears this out (well that's our contention). Rumour has it he moved on to make his other discoveries because he couldn't get a work permit here (now I am kidding).

Chapter 5

Settling In And Setting up

Wally Longbourne was quite simply one of the nicest persons you would ever wish to meet. Large, well over six foot, and massive frame, with kindly eyes and friendly expression that left you in no doubt as to his genuineness. He was commanding and authoritative as well. He had to be. He was Chief Immigration Officer in charge of the entire Islands. He wasted no time in pointing out to us that , as lawyers, we would be eligible under our work permits issued to gain permanent residence in due course, as falling within a category of types of person government was seeking to attract to the Islands. He was also to prove to be a good friend further down the line in the years to come.

Our sponsorship to become members of the Bar was under the auspices of a kindly Canadian lawyer, Fuzzy Drinkmore, and we were duly admitted by the presiding dignitary for such purposes, a distinguished lady called Edna Vintastick. Although retired now to her homeland of Jamaica, this benign lady recently reached her centenary birthday.

I should perhaps preface what follows at this stage to outline our plan. It was simple. Through our law firm contacts we would develop work. We hadn't the faintest notion to expand any local practice which in any case was already amply and well provided for by other law firms. The work in essence would be international in every respect. We also set a budget and a time limit. The idea was to set up as economically as possible and see how things developed.

What we elected for a home and office adjoining was a complete departure and contrast from what we had come from. But it had an appeal to it. Adjoining the Salt Raker Inn on Front Street there were some old but charming premises which rendered themselves ideal for this purpose.

When you opened the front door from the office (the living quarters were at the rear) you walked down a path, through a small garden, to a gate and immediately across the road was the beach and ocean. The casaurina trees fringing the beach side of the road. Every morning a donkey would stop by the gate for a carrot or anything else edible for that matter. The sound of the lapping waves in the morning and gentle surf was idyllic. A far cry from overlooking London Bridge and the Thames perhaps but no less satisfying; in fact more so. This rustic side of life had a definite appeal.

Before I came out to the Islands, I well remember being recommended a book by a well known Parisian tax planning lawyer called Etienne Chouxmeyer, Paradis Fiscaux or something like that. Anyway, it had pictures and for what was normally a fairly stern subject, he had in fact injected an element of humour into it. It showed a photograph set on a beach. A somewhat bald, chubby, smiling bespectacled accountant was seated at his desk there, under the palm trees with the tropical sea behind. On the desk was a typewriter (no computers then) and alongside a cash register. He was drinking a pina colada cocktail and in front of the desk lined up were his snorkel, mask and flippers. The good life! Actually it wasn't quite like that.

And so to basics with the office furniture. In London everything is done for you, of course. We had imported furniture, the type you assemble yourself! The picture on the box depicted some self satisfied seven year old or something assembling the wretched thing in twenty minutes with consummate ease. He had one of those smug looks on his face, like the precocious urchin you used to get on those fruit gums boxes. Three hours later I was still at it. Why is it box instructions have no logic or basic common sense and indulge in incomprehensible jargon of their own (sprockets, enhancing spigots etc). You couldn't even interpret the diagrams! Anyway eventually it was fitted, albeit a bit ski-whiff so to speak. Temperamentally I resembled Donald Duck at his worst.

When it came to paper work, once again there was no immediate supplier for essentials such as standard corporate documents and ingenuity was called for. It came in the strangest format. At this stage I need to introduce Monty Claverhouse into the picture. A former World War Two veteran. Actually that's an understatement by any stretch of the imagination. This fellow had been to Oxford and got the Sword of Honour at Sandhurst Military Academy. But it was his service record that was inspirational.

He was part of special operations which helped evacuate and also sabotage the Germans in their invasion of Crete in 1941. Although it was a debacle for the British, his sort helped mitigate what could have been something far worse and wreaked havoc for the Germans. For them it was probably the most successful airborne parachute invasion in history at that time. Monty was duly honoured. In short this fellow had what it took and was a war hero. What adds credence to it all is the fact that he never voluntarily spoke about it.

After the war he found himself somewhat in the doldrums and couldn't settle. Anyway Monty made a life for himself of sorts in Greece and I have a feeling his writing got him into trouble with the Greek Colonels who instigated the coup there back in 1967. Monty consequently got his marching orders and after trying his hand at various ventures, washed up here as an assistant to the Administrator (Governor).He ran a newspaper, 'The Sea Urchin News', and then as a supplement a printing business which is where I came across him, needing his services. Actually that's not entirely accurate, but pretty much so.

It would help if I describe Monty. About five foot ten tall. Slim, a sleeked back full head of hair. Upright in stature, given his background. His most distinguishing marque, a full blown RAF style handle bar moustache. It was magnificent. Okay, with his lifestyle he had weathered a bit down the years and his nose had a sort of red/ blue veined luminescence to it. I took an instant liking to him and I first met him in the Turks Head Inn. I offered to buy him a drink to which he replied "rather, I am somewhat rather partial to scotch". "What a lot" I politely retorted to which he replied "an understatement dear boy". That was Monty. I must say he stuck manfully to his engagement and produced faultless versions for my memorandum and articles needed for my business. Admittedly we did receive visits for advances of the fees, simply to keep the tanks well topped up as it were!

One anecdote I can never forget was relayed to me by another friend who knew him and this was well before my time there. Monty had been fortunate enough to secure the affections of a Dutch lady who had been a Miss Holland and featured in the Miss World or Universe pageants. They actually got married and she had agreed to live in Grand Turk. Monty had further ideas and responding to a peculiar call of nature had resolved that he and his beloved should try an experimental life living on the uninhabited Island of East Caicos there in the au natural. All there was on East Caicos were cattle and sisal plants and come to think of it a profusion of cacti! Provisions were dropped in weekly by air, but as you can imagine there was not much longevity to be had in this life style. The experiment ended as did Monty's marriage.

A further distinction Monty did have and could add to his curriculum vitae was that he was a fully inducted member of the Knights of the Round Table at the Turks Head Inn. A no mean achievement by anyone's reckoning. This esteemed order consisted of invited attendance at a particular table at the Inn and stood under an old Sappodilla Tree in the garden, where legend had it that magical properties of wisdom were bestowed upon the distinguished Knights gathered below. In short it was the gossip corner. It's attendees were drinking buddies comprising lawyers, accountants and notable characters. The only problem being that the sessions could go on for a lot longer than even the attendees had ever intended. Rumours were very often spawned there just to see how they would go round the Island and get back to them. The father figure at the Table was Patrick O'Shaunnessey, the longest serving lawyer there and who was of considerable importance and whose nay or yea to a number of issues was deemed important if you wanted to succeed in the Islands.

He was personable. Having come to the Islands as Chief Magistrate back in 1964, he was of omniscient importance being, aside from Magistrate, registrar of just about everything (there was no one else) and covered a myriad of functions for which he was deservedly revered. He was head of the Bar Association such as it was. However after some considerable time it was discovered that to be eligible for these roles you had to be a lawyer from either the UK or the Commonwealth, and Ireland, which is where he heralded from ,was clearly not within those domains. On the face of things a gaff had been made. No problem, the laws of eligibility were changed at the drop of a hat and everyone was happy; you could do that in those days, as you weren't harassed by the mindless bureaucracy that pervades everything today.

One amusing note, it was noticed only a few years ago that the normal UK styled insignia shown for the Bar Association depicted a dog, seemingly cocking its leg against the shield, instead of the Unicorn. According to one of the Irish lawyers, it was a follow through adopted from the Irish insignia. It may still be the same today, but nobody really cares!

Chapter 6

Trooping The Brownies And Bring on The Alka Seltzer

Probably the most important invitation of our lives and it came in an unorthodox fashion. It was delivered over the garden fence by Soapy, the cook at the adjoining Salt Raker Inn. The Government delivery boy, although cheerful, couldn't read and letters frequently reached the wrong addressee as a consequence (Government tended to do things like that). And what an invitation! A beautifully embossed gold fringed card with the royal insignia centered with just below. " You are cordially invited to attend the Birthday Celebrations of Her Majesty the Queen at the Parade Ground on Saturday the 12th June at 9am and thereafter to a reception at His Excellency the Governor's residence at Waterloo".

Now let's face it, when I was in London I never received anything of that ilk; "you are cordially invited to Trooping of the Colour at Horse Guards Parade and thereafter to a beano/bash at Buck Pally". And as a seated dignitary at that! Actually just about all British residents received one and of course local personages most importantly. But then, as they say, it's the thought that counts.

So on the appointed morning we duly took ourselves to the Parade Ground about a mile away. Getting there was interesting. Hank and Elise being away, had kindly lent us their transport. It was a battered out old Toyota truck, but for some reason the doors didn't open. So dressed in our ceremonial best we had to clamber in through the windows. Off we trundled at about its top speed of 20mph. Parking at the Parade Ground presented another obstacle, because reverse gear wasn't working and you had to position yourself in such a manner so as always to be able to drive forward. The road there was dusty so we looked as though we had been thrown into the Hovis flour vat when we arrived; the windows didn't wind up or down either and were permanently open as the air conditioning didn't work.

Now another thing has to be kept in mind here. The Islands actually treat Her Majesty's Birthday as a public holiday. Certainly the UK doesn't observe that nor, possibly with the exception of New Zealand (as we later found out from resident Kiwis), does anywhere else.

The Parade Ground itself, actually more or less in the centre of the Island, was a barren open space, partly barb wire fenced, and also served as an impromptu soccer pitch for most of the rest of the time. At one end, sideways on so to speak, there was a pavilion of sorts providing shade from the sun with tiered levels for rows of seats, positioned somewhat ad hoc, where the dignatories would sit.

The ladies in their floppy hats and elegant apparel and the men usually in suits. If you hadn't invested in lighter attire the sweat just poured off you as was the case with London style woolen suits, which most of us had. I noticed a donkey's head protruding through the back of the pavilion, munching on some juicy leaves of a plant growing there. There was a profusion of white handkerchiefs fluttering across the men's faces as they attempted to deal with their sweaty visages.

Larry Looseleaf, the Chief Secretary (which was always a Brit in those days) had the whole protocol off to a tee. Years of experience and he was kitted out in a very smart light white suit, a tie with an emblem on it, and to top a sort of white pork pie hat. Every inch the official; and actually a very nice one at that; having even been inducted as an honorary member of the Knights of the Round Table. Around the perimeter of the Parade Ground were an assembly of locals and other expats, interspersed at intervals with the odd donkey or cow grazing at the verges where the grass ended.

Pride of place of course went to the Governor, representing Her Majesty. He had arrived in a white London taxi. Out front of the pavilion on the Parade Ground was a white pedestal (it actually looked like an upturned painted orange box and probably was) for him to take the salute of the subsequent march past. He had white dubboned boots, razor sharp creased white trousers and a white tunic. The latter curiously without a belt; perhaps so as to not convey so much of a military bearing. Persil would have been proud of him. His collar and epaulettes were adorned with ceremonial egg. Whilst his white pith helmet had feathers sprouting out at the top; its appearance resembling something along the lines of an ostrich's upturned bottom. Nowadays they just wear grey lounge suits. This was truly the vestiges of Empire. But the poor fellow must have felt the heat; he reminded you a bit of the actor Terry Thomas who used to play that type of role in the old Ealing Studios film comedies.

At first he turned to the assembly announcing various honours and gongs that had been awarded in celebration of Her Majesty's Birthday. Unfortunately the acoustics weren't good coupled with the fact that there was a sporadic wind across the Parade Ground. It sounded very distant, like someone talking through a hat pulled over his head. Once over he turned to the open Parade Ground and the march past began.

Now alright we don't exactly have the massed bands of the Household Division, nor the five Regiments of Foot Guards or the Household Cavalry for that matter, but we make up for that in our own special quaint way, and no less effectively I might add. Heading the ensemble was the Royal Turks and Caicos Police Band. A resplendent if not somewhat motley crew of gentlemen and lady officers of various sizes. With white tunics if a bit rumpled, heavy brogued shoes, gentlemen with dark blue trousers with red striped sides and the ladies sporting heavy skirts and thick dark stockings; a bit reminiscent of Soviet track and field officials or 1970's hostesses on Bulgarian Airlines. The hats flat topped with a protruding sun visor at front and sorely needed. They mustered about fifteen and their instruments had been donated by a Texan millionaire who had bailed out and taken over the recently bankrupted national airline.

Their rendition? Well not exactly the Royal Bahamian Police Band by a long shot and it might even have had Sousa crying but all in all not bad. Probably more in the mode of the Monty Python themed effort with the odd hiccup and misfired note. To coin a P.G. Wodehouse expression "what a splendid noise".

Following them came non-musical police with shouldered Lee Enfield rifles, an assortment of the British Legion, Boys Brigade, Scouts, Girl Guides, and the Brownies with their bright yellow scarves; in some cases toddlers lead by the hand. There might even have been a casually stray donkey following up, so that took care of the Household Cavalry bit. Throughout this procession the Governor took the salute steadfast and upright, chin elevated at forty-five degrees. Beat that Horse Guards Parade! Then it was off to Waterloo for the entertainment side of things. The Governor's party was always something to look forward to in those days. By contrast today's efforts (with austerity and the like) rank as positively anemic efforts by comparison. Whilst decorum was generally polite and well observed you could usually measure the success of these do's by counting the number of close on horizontal inebriated souls left as the casualties at their conclusion; Governor possibly included.

The nosh was well catered for as well. All in all they were great fun. One reason for this and perhaps a star of the show was the chief bar tender, Police Sergeant Sylvester Plonkit, whose drink measures were gargantuan. When he held a glass to the upturned dispensing bottle, it was as if he had a perpetual case of St. Vitus's dance in his hands. Whopping and lethal cocktails. The noise levels of laughter rose as did the slurring of speech in the victims.

He was an interesting character. Always smiling, diminutive with a huge General Kitchener style moustache. His career in the force seemed to endure fluctuating fortunes. Having at various times held the ranks of corporal, superintendent and back to sergeant. Rumour had it that on one occasion his demotion followed his attempted use of the Force to eject his wife from the matrimonial home during a domestic dispute. Whatever, he was the life and soul of the party and always readily shaking your hand whenever you met him and exchanging pleasantries.

At the end of the festivities (well, the point at which we couldn't take any more food and drink and being some eight hours later when it was pitch dark) climbing into the truck rather than a conventional entry seemed natural given my state.

By the way we were by far the last to leave; the veterans getting well into their stride. Somehow you always get home. And it helped that encountering any car or pedestrian was a rarity at that time. Still drinking at that level was an anathema to me then and we were just pleased to get home without episode. They have only recently introduced drinking laws in the Islands which are enforced, but I am pretty sure that had I blown into a breathalyzer on that occasion, I would have floated over the roof tops like something out of Mary Poppins.

How is it that something you love so much can treat you so badly the next morning? I certainly had never had a hangover of that magnitude, perhaps not even in my student days. You wake up, if you can call it that. More like coming round after an operation. Opening ones eyes, the sunlight is of course searing in like lasers. The top of your skull feels as if it has been surgically removed so that your brain is openly being incinerated by its rays. You stagger to the bathroom and look at what passes for a non-alien form in the mirror. Eyes like tomatoes in a bowl of custard. Your mouth feels like the bottom of a parrot's cage. Your tongue, a piece of sandpaper. You get the drift. Never again (that is until the next time!).

Worse still, I actually had a day ahead of me. Today I took delivery of my transport. It was called the Green Goddess; a 1962 Cadillac. This needs explaining. Cars were not the most easily acquired commodities in the Islands in those days and you pretty much had to take whatever you could get. As it turned out I was lucky (well we'll stick with that expression for the time being), Chris Spivling, a British guy employed by the local aviation authority had come to the end of his contract and was being repatriated to the U.K. He owned this car. In its own way it must have been a magnificent specimen in its hey day. Supremely comfortable. In fact it was rather like going around on a motorized sofa. And gadgetry galore. Air conditioning of course, but even a light sensor dimming switch on its dashboard; which caused the lights to automatically dip when sensing oncoming traffic. It had a big V-8 engine which propelled it with powerful surges. Actually the latter gave you a clue as to some of its foibles or 'Genevieve' like traits so to speak. This car almost had a mind of its own. To clear the valves and open up the car he used to go hairing down the Grand Turk airport runway, when no planes were coming of course. He could do that, or did anyway. Try doing that down Heathrow's main runway!

It actually looked like the Batmobile, with protruding fins at the rear. It was fun to drive even if impractical. It gobbled fuel. The gauge almost visibly dropping as you drove. One night, having been invited to dinner at friends up on the Ridge, I applied the throttle going up the hill and it roared into life. Trouble was it didn't stop. The pedal seemed stuck and we flew along the Ridge, swerved into our friends driveway, like something out of the Rockford files, whilst I jammed down on the brakes. We were almost in the pool when it stopped. Just like that, to quote Tommy Cooper. Shaken we went into dinner amidst astonished looks from our hosts. I could swear the radiator grill had an extended grin on it.

The corollary to this adventure happened the next morning, when peering under the bonnet (hood to our American friends) in a forlorn attempt to detect the problem, when Monty happened along clutching his customary book and puffing his perpetual cigarette. He asked if he might be of assistance, mentioning that vehicles were a feature of his past in Crete when he had to get things running or face capture, often facing seemingly insurmountable problems.

He ducked under the hood and muttered WD-40. Off he

mozied and came back with a can of the stuff within about half an hour. The throttle cable had become rusted and stuck and good old WD-40 was the cure for this as a lubricant. I was later to learn that this blessed substance was virtually a panacea to so many mechanical problems that arose on an Island. So grateful I asked if I could repay him somehow, but of course he declined and simply wanted a lift further downtown which I was more than happy to oblige with.

When we got to his destination, which was after a few minutes, I was puzzled where he was going, but assumed that as an old hand to the place there were a myriad of nooks and crannies and places of interest which a greenhorn like myself would be ignorant of. He ruminated for a little while and then pointed across the road to an old disused building. Somehow it didn't look as if it had ever been a home.

"I was a prisoner once" he said. "What in Crete" seemed the ensuing logic of it. "No here, actually and I was kidnapped", he retorted. I simply had to know more and then he recounted his tale. It was back in 1976, round about the time the Islands gained their constitution encouraging a level of self government. There were all sorts of political shenanigans going on and matters could get a little heated. Having said as much, you have to bear in mind that we are talking of a small community here, so that a lot of what may seem serious is really a storm in a teacup as it were. A very charismatic leader called Jags McCartney had emerged and was pretty well respected and was fighting for the rights of locals. He eventually emerged as the Islands first Chief Minister in what was then the first system of Ministerial Government.

Anyway the essence of the plot was that some demonstration was called for and a group of protestors decided to kidnap someone and hold them to ransom until their demands were satisfied. Occasional shots were fired, but frankly no one was aiming at anyone and the whole purpose was just to make a loud protest.

The kidnap victim was, you guessed it, Monty, as he happened to be wandering past at the time and he was imprisoned (if that's the right term) in a bar called the Junkanoo Club, whilst a standoff ensued with the Authorities. Being a bar and on his own admission Monty was a very happy kidnap victim and happily whiled away the couple of days this escapade lasted. In fact his most alarming moment was when agreement was reached and the siege ended, and Monty was forced to part from his dungeon of inebriation. So much for the theme of booze.

Chapter 7

What's It All About, Alfie?

Alfie was one of my favorite characters of my Grand Turk days. He and his lovely and very capable wife, Esmarelda, owned and operated what was known as The Ramparts. Amongst other things it figured as the Island's main supermarket, if you can describe it as such. Certainly it was nothing that would have worried the Tesco chain or featured in its advertising.

The food plane, a very old and noisy Douglas prop DC-6, brought the food in every Wednesday. Its arrival was something like the equivalent of Wishbone, the cook in the Raw Hide western series, sounding the dinner triangle and shouting "Come and get it". We would all flock to the stores like a plague of locusts. The provisions therefore had to be speedily unloaded and stacked on the store shelves in readiness for this onslaught.

Alfie and Esmarelda had a somewhat unique split of their business interests in the store. Certain provisions, say meats, were Alfie's and the other half, for example veggies and canned items, were Esmarelda's. It was to be strictly adhered to. Each had separate cash registers opposite each other at the exit and woe betide anyone who usurped this peculiar arrangement, by taking the wrong item to the wrong allotted cash register.

There was a healthy element of competition which arose and perhaps sometimes the occasional altercation between them, as to which items fell into their respective categories of responsibility and ownership. Now I bet you never encountered that at your local supermarket. At the end of each day they totted up their takings and toddled off home together carrying their respective earnings. We had no taxes or reporting requirements then, so strict accounting wasn't mandatory except perhaps between themselves. They each had their own internal fortress so to speak, or more perhaps more aptly, a 'Berlin Wall'.

The Ramparts, as indeed the name implies, was a very sturdy off white building comprising very heavy stonework. It was a rabbit warren and maze of different rooms and Alfie was always altering things internally, for reasons which I never fully understood. Getting lost was a distinct possibility. The supermarket was actually at the back, facing Pond Street, whilst the remaining rooms tended towards Front Street and the sea. There were a number of residential tenants and two law firm offices upstairs facing the sea. One end comprising the chambers of Jasper Stoneyheart, a former attorney general to the Islands, and now in private practice. The other end occupied by Alonso Rolly, a Jamaican lawyer recently come to the Islands. In the supermarket, Alfie and Esmarelda were assisted by Miss. Tilly a diligent elderly lady and a Haitian called "Biscuit". Both Alfie and Biscuit conversed in a sort of pigeon style banter, which frankly no one else ever seemed to understand, but obviously they did and it worked.

Alfie was in his mid-sixties then and stood about five foot six. Although balding, his head was covered in grey bristles and his cheeks and chin as well. He had a congenial face with dark penetrating brown eyes. Given that he was Jamaican and having lived in the Islands since at least the 1950's, it always struck me how white he was, without any trace of a tan. He always wore a short sleeve shirt, casual slacks and sandals.

I don't think dentistry was a strong feature in his life because save for a few upper teeth he seemingly had a single prominent tooth in his lower jaw. He had that lovely Jamaican drawl accent you come across, but with his tooth impediment it tended to become a little indistinct as to what he was actually saying, sometimes with comical results. Like when at Christmas time he telephoned me saying his beers had come in, which it turned out were teddy bears for presents. It reminded me a bit of Benny Hill misreading the news.

As mentioned Alfie had come to the Islands with the Jamaican Government back in the early fifties (as the Islands were administered by Jamaica in those days, Jamaica being a colony of the U.K. then.) I would guess that he turned his hand to importing and groceries sometime around the late fifties/ early sixties. He developed an intense interest in the history of the Islands and subsequently wrote four volumes which he had published. It was illustrated and took the form of an anecdotal style, which actually made for very interesting reading as it came up with nuances and details you might not ordinarily find in a more conventional compilation. He put a lot of work into it down the years and it was one of the very few sources as to the history of the Islands, it was fascinating and I still frequently reference my copies of it. In short, he stood as our local historian and deservedly so.

He did some of the earliest work as a proponent of the first Columbus landfall in the New World being Grand Turk. He had visited libraries in Spain. Researched data and discovered how Columbus, some thirty years later on his death bed, had narrated the story of his first voyage to Navaratti, a monk who wrote it down. The theory is compelling .

Alfie was also a true raconteur and his stories were mesmerizing. Above all else he liked to have fun. I had a notion that Alfie's aspirations in this regard were always somewhat put on hold and restrained by Esmarelda (perhaps, understandably so and probably in his own best interests) and that whilst she was on Island his domestic life was somewhat more tranquil and orthodox. But when Esmarelda went off Island, as frequently happened, to stay at their home in Miami, well he would let his hair down (actually not literally as he had none). He reminded me a bit of the character of Toad in The Wind in the Willows. As soon as the cat was away the mouse (Alfie) would put out the call to all his buddies to rally round for a session of serious rum drinking and general whooping it up at his very nice house up on the Ridge.

We somehow found ourselves included in this distinguished retinue and I still cannot get out of my mind one story he told; probably because I am not sure as to its veracity and whether it was the rum or Alfie talking. Esmarelda liked occasionally to go on holidays on her own, probably a much needed break and from Alfie as well. However Alfie had taken to the notion that she was engrossed in some liaison with another party and believing as such he had resolved to get to the bottom of it. I must stress again, this was from the horses own mouth!

Finding that she had booked a holiday in Buenos Aires, he took himself off there ahead of Esmerada's arrival. Reaching the hotel where she was scheduled to arrive , he took up a disguise in the form of a black curly wig and a moustache curled up at the ends. He obtained employment as a bell hop and consequently was attired in the uniform and gained access to her bedroom just before she arrived. He hid in the wardrobe for a time and upon hearing her entering the room he jumped out of the wardrobe to confront her, presumably expecting to find an embarrassed eloping pair of lovers. Alas, no such eventuality. He maintained there was someone with her but clearly his timing and plan had gone awry.

Anyway our budding Sherlock Holmes returned home with his tail between his legs as it were. Personally, although he swore to its efficacy, I think it was pure balderdash. But you have to admit it made for a very good story. You wonder what their expression must have been like when he alighted from the wardrobe in such dramatic fashion, if it had been true.

As to getting home from his very nice house on the ridge, we were presented with somewhat of a dilemma. The Green Goddess being out of action, Alfie had kindly brought us. However he was pretty well comatose with rum by the time we had to go, so we found ourselves getting a ride back with Ronnie Flounder and Don Waddling. Ronnie had a local import and freight agency and Don represented the interests of a Greek company (fearing tax changes in Greece they had built about the only modern complex on the Islands as a contingency measure if they had to evacuate Greece. It was some three stories high but virtually empty and right next to the airport).

Ronnie and Don weren't in much better condition than Alfie, but insisted on driving, notwithstanding my offer as I was somewhat sober by comparison after the last outing. Both men were in their late fifties and easy going, but as inducted members of the Round Table well, the effects were beginning to show. Both being quite portly and ruddy faced and passed their prime so to speak.

They weren't even sure whose car it was, let alone who was driving. The vehicle was very old (I am sure something of fifties vintage) and they had trouble starting it. It actually had one of those old crank shaft handles which you had to turn. So whilst we sat anxiously in the back seat, they both staggered out and for some unknown reason together tried turning the handle , wobbling as they stood. Trouble was they were trying different ways and both flew off in different directions only to crawl back and try again. It eventually worked and the old engine sparked to life and they both literally crawled back into the car, with Don the designated driver, if you can call it that.

He somehow couldn't see well and decided the windscreen needed a wipe. He went to the boot (trunk to our North American friends) and brought out his means of wiping. It turned out to be a dead chicken, with its feathers still on which someone had obviously given him. He commenced wiping haphazardly with his face pressed against the windscreen, looking something like Quasimodo. Once done we set off, the chicken on his lap.

What was normally a five minute journey took about forty minutes. And Ronnie even tried to alight from the car at one stage, thinking we had arrived. We must have been crawling at about 2mph all the way, meandering from one side of the road to the other. Somehow we arrived and thankfully got out, leaving them to chug on to their respective destinations. Our day out at Alfie's having concluded.

Looking back, I have little doubt that Alfie and Esmarelda were very fond of each other, since when she died a few years later he was like a rudderless ship. He did move on so to speak, which brings to mind another venture he embarked upon.

Being lonely he decided to advertise in the press for a secretary and assistant. Not locally you understand, but in the Canadian press. The advert ran something like: "Sophisticated Caribbean Millionaire requires the services of a young attractive secretary to assist in research work, very lucrative pay and working conditions." Not surprisingly the bait had some takers. Problem was when they arrived. Apart from seeing Grand Turk, when they saw Alfie eagerly awaiting them off the plane, rubbing his hands with invisible soap (and probably discerning his true intentions) they invariably returned or as in one case stuck with the same plane for its return journey. Alas, Alfie the lothario it was deemed not to be.

Chapter 8

Hurricanes Hardly Ever Happen

In Hertford, Herefordshire and Hampshire hurricanes hardly ever happen, so goes that wonderful tune from the musical *My Fair Lady*; a take-off of Shaw's *Pygmalian*. Well, having lived in Hertford once, I can certainly attest to that. I can also attest to having experienced Hurricane Kate which hit the Islands back in 1985. Late in the season as it happened, and believe me this is one female you can well do without.

Having just recently been through Hurricane Irma and to a lesser extent Maria, there is one modern innovation we should all be truly grateful for and that is the satellite systems. Their early warning service truly saves lives that would otherwise be lost. Back in 1985 we had no such help and what you got in the way of advanced warning was often through Miami's weather and airport tracking systems as relayed from there and, as happened in our case, via the pilots who flew into the Islands. Our warning in this instance actually came second hand.

It's a strange feature of hurricanes (and again some indicator of their imminent approach) that clouds which normally lazily drift by suddenly start streaming off altogether in a particular direction. As if part of a gigantic cycle, which in fact is what hurricanes are. It's weird to watch and of course the skies start to darken.

I was outside the office looking across at the sea, when Jasper Stoneyheart the lawyer, who liked to swim with his Labrador just there, came out of the water and mentioned that he had bumped into a pilot earlier that morning and who mentioned that Miami was forecasting a grade 2 strength hurricane (now named Kate) to be heading our way. So preparations, and quick ones at that, were the order of the day. Living at the Ramparts, all that was necessary was for Biscuit to put down the shutters for them, to weather the impending storm.

It struck me as a bit odd that not more widespread knowledge of this emergency wasn't doing the rounds as it were. Jasper simply said "you might ask that twit supposedly in charge at Waterloo, but don't bank on anything". Now at this somewhat irreverent reference to the Governor, I had better elaborate a little more at this stage about Jasper; he also figures later in this segment.

Jasper had up until about three years previously been the attorney general for the Islands; Government's lawyer if you like. On coming to the end of his contract he had stayed on and elected to start a law practice of his own. Governor's had changed meanwhile and the current incumbent had taken exception to this on the grounds that there was a perceived conflict of interest in Jasper starting up so soon.

Consequently something akin to a war ensued and given the parochial smallness of the place it resembled something along the lines of a Hillys and the Billys shootout. With metaphoric salvos in the form of writs, law suits and other diatribe flowing to and forth between Waterloo and the

Ramparts via the courts. In short they cordially loathed one another and it must have been awkward for the then current attorney general, Duncan Cockalot, who found himself in the middle of this dueling.

Problem for the Government side of things was that Jasper seemed to enjoy a considerable degree of success as a result of these skirmishes and unfortunately was given to somewhat upping his finger at the Waterloo establishment whenever the opportunity arose (actually a bad habit, because city hall always has the resources to win in the end). Unpleasantly for the Governor, Jasper had the nasty habit of suing the Governor personally (something any civil servant would turn bleached white at with dread at such a prospect)) and a Crown Proceedings law was introduced as a measure of protection. In fact I have never seen legislation enacted so quickly in my life. Anyway it gives you a backdrop to the situation.

I decided to call the Governor's Office and I actually got him personally and he was eager to be informative about the forthcoming storm. He immediately told me that he was alright and safely bunkered down in his shelter and everything at the Governor's residence and office had been boarded up. His cogent advice to me was to get out of where I was quickly as there was a life threatening possibility of flooding, being at the sea front.

He then proceeded to recount his experiences in the Gilbert and Ellice Islands in the Pacific, where they had the equivalent of what are called typhoons. At one juncture I politely asked what about the rest of the Islands preparedness for this seeming forthcoming disaster. At which he paused and said he wasn't quite sure what the rest of the island had done, as there hadn't been time to address anything else other than his own immediate predicament. For a moment it conjured up for me the vision of a sinking ship and instead of the captain being the last over the rail, in fact being the first to grab a life raft! I left it at that and started thinking about what to do.

Our place was well over a hundred years old and must have endured this sort of thing before. Flooding was the most likely problem assuming the roof held. So scores of towels were jammed into every possible opening around the place and anything of value stacked as high as possible; we were quite lucky in that regard as there was plenty of space. We then made sure that we had other essentials such as batteries, torches, water, canned food supplies. Candles for when the power would go off, which for safety reasons could be at any time. By today's reckoning these are crude preparations but then it was a case of whatever you could think of.

If there is one thing I hate about hurricanes it is that for some reason they always seem to hit at night time. Not that it made much difference, but somehow it seemed more psychologically reassuring if it came during daylight. Daft I know and in any event we had old heavy wooden louvred shutters that came down over the windows, so it was quite dark in any event.

Just as we thought about as much could be done as possible the telephone rang. It was Alfie, insisting we came up to his place to ride out the storm. Thanking him, he arrived about half an hour later and with essentials such as overnight things, passports and other valuables we made it to his place.

It's quite difficult to describe the hurricane when it hits. The wind and rain build up into a howling raging crescendo. The walls and windows surge almost with the onslaught and of course lesser structures are destroyed. You certainly don't sleep unless you happen to be drunk, which some did tell me that that was precisely what they did. Pretty foolish if matters do get serious, as you need to be able to cope. What is curious is that after the storm has raged at its seeming maximum, everything goes very still and quiet and it gets very hot, then the whole raging commences again. That is because you experience the eye going over, so in effect you get the front and back of the hurricane. Whoever you are, it is an experience that leaves you shaken.

In the morning you witness an aftermath of chaos and destruction. Vegetation is ravaged, trees felled lying across roads and having destroyed houses. Roofs torn off and buildings having collapsed. Power lines down. Wetness pervades everywhere. How the wild animals survive it is bewildering, but they do and they seem to have a strange sense as to when storms are coming well before we are aware of them; with an uncanny knack of finding cover of some sort.

Thanking Alfie for his kindness, we decamped and were taken back where we were surprised and delighted to find everything really in tact. Some flooding yes. The main victim had been the garden, but it is astonishing how plant life surges back after these events and after a few weeks that proved to be the case. Power came back on after about a week.

We suddenly remembered that we were about to receive some international clients, about a week after the hurricane. Through London contacts we ended up representing a renowned Middle Eastern prince who, being engaged in a substantial project in Europe, had formed a number of companies with us for that purpose. Probably not even being aware where the Turks and Caicos Islands were he wanted his trusted lieutenants to check out where his companies were located and perhaps for want of better description find out, well, that we were genuine.

His entrusted emissaries were his personal lawyer Abdul Lafoul and Sir Cuthbert Askewnoll, ex British Ambassador to

Egypt and a close family friend of the Prince and his family. They were booked in at the Kittina Hotel along the road. What it lacked in five star luxury, it made up for in Caribbean character and friendliness and quite honestly was not unpleasant and in any event about the best we could come up with. They were extremely nice people and actually found our premises quaint. Having satisfied themselves as to our bona fides and that the companies really did exist, it only remained for us to have recourse to dinner.

The only problem was that as an ongoing restaurant after the hurricane, the only truly functional restaurant was Le Papillon; the little place buttressing out into the sea and run by Pierre Lagouste and his common law wives. It had survived with a slight uplifting of the corrugated iron roofing, but with little hurricane lamps and rustic tables it had the appeal of a small bistro with low lighting hiding any other imperfections.

They seemed to like the atmosphere. We were at a square table facing one another and just as we had circulated the only menu, a cockroach chose to run down the middle of the table and over the butter palette, thereafter to disappear into the kitchen , where a cat could be seen licking something. They both laughed which eased our horrified faces. The food was tasty and the question of dessert arose. The large roley poley waitress who served us lumbered over to take our orders. Our guests both wanted profiteroles with cream. She looked into the air and said somewhat drily "they 're' all gone, he had the last one over there" pointing to some harmless and now acutely embarrassed diner across the other side of the room. Fait accomplis, as it were. It was apple tart instead.

At about this juncture who should wade into the restaurant but Jasper and his wife Elaine. Jasper dressed in a formal white dinner jacket, somewhat at odds with his surroundings. My best description of Jasper would be to say that he looked like a tall version of Alec Guinness acting as George Smiley in the Le Carre books. Abdul took me by the sleeve and whispered "goodness, is that the Governor dressed like that? "No, far from it actually" I said. Amazingly, after Abdul and Sir Cuthbert had departed, the report back later on was favourable. They had thoroughly enjoyed their experience in what was an interesting little place!

One episode always sticks in my mind post that hurricane. I recall having a coffee at Ray Bridenorth's (the engineer) apartment in Duke Street a few days later. Visiting him and his wife Mary was a young English character off a yacht. Apparently after the storm he had been engaged with others salvaging a yacht and somehow a piece of machinery had fallen and actually severed half his foot off. It was bandaged and obviously medical attention had been administered at the local hospital. It was an appalling injury and what an awful legacy for him. He was very cheerful and upbeat and did he need it. I truly wished him well and hope all worked out fine after he left the Islands.

Before Kate the last hurricane to cause devastation was Donna in 1960 and we were not to receive anything really serious until 2008 when Hurricane Ike struck. That was category 4 in force. Irma ranked the mother of them all at category 5 and no one ever here wants to see the like again. The cost and devastation of these things are enormous. What does restore faith is the sheer guts and resilience of the human spirit to deal with these events. And at traumatic times like that you tend to see, for the most part, the very best of people.

Chapter 9

Pan Am And Some Discarded Wrecks

Walking to the post office was always a delight. Not that we got much post; about two visits a week became the norm, coinciding with the inbound flights to the Islands. Especially in the morning, when to with start you had the marvelous glitter of the sun off the sea and the lapping waves. After about two hundred yards there was the enchanting avenue (actually called Duke Street and leading into Front Street) and then Front Street itself with that historic arc of old ramshackle buildings stretching for about a quarter of a mile to the dock. The post office was half way along there.

At the start of Duke Street stood the Turks Head Inn and on this particular occasion, about 11am, out popped Fuzzy Drinkmore who had had his customary first knockings so to speak. "Pan Am, Pan Am, they 're coming here" he exclaimed. "Inaugural flight, Sunday, be there". He was very close to me and had I had a lit cigar in my mouth, we would both have been incinerated; his breath being the equivalent of high octane. He ambled back to his office, leaving me to ruminate on this momentous piece of news.

The nice thing about Fuzzy was that he was always in good

humour. When I first visited his office he gave me his brochure and its title had a misprint under his firms name 'Turks and Caos Islands' (just missing the 'h'). Whether that was a Freudian slip or a simple typo who knows. It was definitely to prove prophetic. Fuzzy was always well turned out in a casual sort of way. His most unusual feature being that I don't think I have met anyone with their eyes set so close together. You almost went cross eyed yourself when making eye contact. Anyway, Sunday was to be marked out as a special inauguration day. We had finally arrived on the world map.

The Green Goddess, still being out of action, I took my bicycle for the mile and a half trip down the dusty road leading to the airport. Going round the southern perimeter I spotted the plane already having landed; set in splendid isolation as it were. Gleaming in its livery, with the Pan Am insignia above the blue flashing below. It somehow represented one of those moments which James Joyce described as an epiphany or aesthetic experience (Okay, a bit much, but you take my meaning). Everything around it was dwarfed by this seemingly brand new Airbus. The contrast of the old and the new. The future for the Islands!

I always liked Pan Am anyway, in fact let's be more poignant, I liked flying then. People and airlines were nice and you felt special. Marked contrast with today's cattle truck philosophy of shipping you en masse with the maximum of stress. Nowadays the airlines treat you like a piece of cargo they once contracted to carry and now wish they hadn't. The amazing thing is that more people are flying than ever! You can almost feel the waves of hate or at best indifference from their executives as they seek to nickel and dime you at every turn of the travelling screw. Forever increasing your discomfort to cut costs and maximize profit. In fairness, the actual staff you encounter are pleasant.

Pan Am as it turned out proved the saviour and catalyst to the Islands development. And we were lucky to have them for some five years before sadly they went under in late 1990. The staff were exceedingly nice as well. Often upgrading you because you were a resident or onboard giving you a bottle of wine if left over at the end of the flight. You actually felt like going somewhere. Suddenly more people knew where we were. Up until then we had had a series of smaller airlines providing a service which just wasn't viable for them, but they were greatly appreciated.

As I gazed back towards the road to go home a car happened to pass me and the occupants gave a wave. It was the Discardi brothers, Oswald and Leopold, typically in a car that would have been condemned anywhere else. But it worked and was cheap, which was pretty much their principal criterion for just about everything. The one must have been picking the other up off the inaugural flight. They had become good friends of ours and perhaps a more unusual pair of siblings you would never come across in your entire life.

They heralded from Jamaica and I have an inkling that their Jewish ancestors had migrated there at least three generations back from Lebanon. The Caribbean has a lot of Lebanese people and they are renowned as financiers and successful business people. They had both been immensely successful there in business and I believe owned a stake in one of the largest food processing companies called Lascelles, which was publicly quoted.

Oswald was the older of the two by about four years. He had a slight stature and a wizened and sagacial look about him which in fact reflected a very shrewd financial acumen. Leopold was taller, over six foot, and had a distinguished upright bearing to his gait, with a thick head of hair always neatly groomed well back from his forehead. Leopold was often to be seen walking down Duke Street with his dog; he had a penchant for Afghan Hounds, a far cry from our native potcake dog variety. They were both highly educated and I often wondered what on earth brought two characters of this stature to the Islands.

Apparently in the early seventies Jamaica had experienced political upheaval with leanings to the left and this had impacted with the unions on businesses there. Fearful of draconian control in the pipeline, both brothers had decided to extricate themselves and to whatever extent possible (I suspect a lot) their fortunes out of Jamaica. This was no easy task as Jamaica had exchange control, but such was the extent of their dealings overseas that suitable prospects arose to enable them to achieve this. Hence they came to Grand Turk , which was near, and the parent company had a subsidiary of sorts in Grand Turk, which they now elected to conveniently operate.

By now you will have gathered that 'antiquated' rates as a serious theme for Grand Turk. But if there were Oscar awards for this, then the Discardi Brothers would win outright, not a contender in sight. Their business H.Q. was just beyond the dock on Front Street, about a hundred yards up to the right. A large old wooden warehouse of a building, the wood could have come straight from Noah's Ark it was so ancient. At the front there were enormous doors to cater for any object imported to be housed and piles of goods were haphazardly stacked up to the ceiling.

It had an office, but to reach it you had to ascend some rickety old stairs running outside of the building to a height of some twenty five feet and steeply inclined. How Leopold, who manned the office, managed to go up and down those each day defies belief, because some stairs were missing and there was a general sense of rotting when you looked at their supportive strength. He had to be at least in his sixties. I did it once and felt that I fully deserved the George Cross; even if awarded posthumously, as was a distinct possibility. The office itself was like something out of Dickens's Bleak House. Piles of dusty ledgers, I may even have spotted a quill pen. Air conditioning was deemed an expensive luxury so whoever was in the office had a Victorian equivalent of a sauna. The only concession to the twentieth century being a telephone.

They also had a little food provisions shop about halfway down Front Street. It was a stark whitewashed building with really no eye to presentation. Leopold often complained that its shoppers, who were few, had a habit of breaking the sealed vacuum on food and jam jars. Taking a scooped finger of the contents to taste and if not to their liking recapping the jar and replacing it on the shelf. A conscientious consumer no doubt, but it drove the brothers understandably wild; especially when an unsuspecting customer brought their purchase back. The meat selection was not for the faint hearted and it brought back memories of a Kandy open meat market I once wandered into when I was in Sri Lanka. Say no more!

Notwithstanding their somewhat parsimonious life style, both Oswald and Leopold were conscientious and very courteous. Their domestic situation simply reflected one of convenience. Both had seen life. I don't think Oswald had ever married and at one time Leopold had been to a very attractive blonde English girl, who endured living in Grand Turk for as long as she could. But eventually she had had enough and understandably needed more from life than living in a vast shack with both brothers on a shoe string budget.

The house she left was situated in Duke Street and set well back from the road. In fact it was literally in part over the sea itself. Erosion having occurred, so that the lounge was actually undercut by the tide and at one corner the property was tipping into the sea. Neither brother saw any cogent reason to correct this precarious situation. It would prove expensive. Someone once even suggested, albeit somewhat uncharitably, that they probably had burglar alarms on their dustbins!

Oswald and Leopold had a unique way of replacing their transport. When a vehicle wouldn't go any further it was simply left in the front garden to rot away. I counted at least four of these forlorn rusting heaps. It seemed a practical expedient to them.

They could be extremely generous and on one occasion kindly let us use their apartment in North Miami Beach; in fact quite close to the Aventura Mall in what was a very fashionable area of Miami. It was probably built in the seventies and they had a nice penthouse apartment on the twenty-sixth floor. For shopping it was sheer manna from heaven and the stay was enjoyable to the nth degree. Save for one curious episode. One afternoon there was a knock on the door and the concierge, who was very polite, needed to show us something. It was causing a considerable dilemma for the complex management.

He took us down to the garage beneath the building to what was the allocated parking spot that went with the apartment we were staying in. In front of us was a Fiat sports car, it's suspension having collapsed and its wheels splayed out in a rusting heap! Could we help in any way, because whilst the owners promptly paid all outgoings by banking order, it was proving impossible to contact them and they scarcely ever visited. It seems the vehicle had been bought years earlier, brand new, and then just left to rot. Had we ever seen anything like it. Yes we said, actually we have.

When Leopold, the surviving brother, died his probated estate was quoted at $44 million! The passing of the likes of

Oswald, Leopold, Alfie and Monty, many years ago now, saw the end of an era. They had formed part of the Islands rich pageant of eccentrics and personalities, which quite simply we no longer have anymore. They are irreplaceable and gone as are their homes and businesses. It is perhaps a far cry from the trends of today where we are forever bombarded with impersonal technology taking over our lives with the almost robotic pursuit of mindless rules and regulations. What these old friends had was individuality of thought and humanity, however batty they may have seemed at the time. My life was certainly the richer for it and I wouldn't have missed it for the world.

Chapter 10

Where The Sun Never Sets

Probably at this juncture it is beholden to explain how the Islands were governed (or not, according to your point of view). The words in parenthesis not being a jibe, because for years everything was so simple and everything just ticked by, applying resourcefulness and a little common sense where appropriate. It was bliss, with an absence of the bureaucracy which now prevails.

We are what is popularly but incorrectly termed a British colony, the correct identification being British Overseas Dependent Territory. There are about fourteen of them left now around the world; the vestiges of what was the almighty British Empire. I well remember at school looking at an atlas and noting that a third of the world's landmass being coloured red , denoting this imperial fact. How times have changed.

As such we are under the ultimate control of the Crown, Her Majesty's Government; specifically the Foreign and Commonwealth Office, designated FCO from hereon, as they call themselves. Have ever you noticed the in vogue, almost obsession, with acronyms nowadays; government departments, company names, organizations. It's as if someone has swallowed a scrabble board. My theory being that it all follows an Orwellian 1984 impersonalization process besetting our world today i.e. eviscerate any character from life and leaving us all beholden to Big Brother. O.K. back to the point.

Within this framework, and since 1976, we have a Constitution (although in more recent times it has been replaced), which provides for an internally elected government (with supporting civil service), consisting of Chief Minister (nowadays called Premier), cabinet colleagues, other members of Government and an opposition, all under the auspices of the Governor , who has his representative as well. The whole idea being to encourage self government for as and when the Islands break from the apron strings of mother U.K. and go independent. The latter being a development the U.K. end of things is committed towards, under its United Nations accords.

There are reserved powers for the Governor, such as defense, international matters impacting on the Islands, policing, security and with an overall power to step in if cause is deemed necessary. Basically the U.K. is meant to be doing itself out of a job and relinquishing power eventually.

So far so good. But In reality for years the FCO took very little interest in the Islands and they carried on in their slow peaceful, tortoise like way. There is good reason for this. Put bluntly we are really an anachronism to them as they are not sure what to do with the place save wait for independence. You see we are no longer a strategic outpost guarding sea lanes and being of importance during their wars with the French, Spanish, Dutch and the Americans centuries ago. We have become a political irrelevance.

We are a quaint backwater; rather like that small parochial village of Clochemerle, in the novel of that name. This is in stark contrast to the colonies belonging still to the French and

Dutch; who regard their territories almost as extensions of themselves. With consequent greater interest being taken with investment and infrastructure and a meaningful participation in their welfare. The term not infrequently used for us has been 'benign neglect".

In practical terms this parody and how Government operates often mirrors that wonderful U.K. comedy "Yes Prime Minister". With successive Governors and their officials acting out roles akin to Sir Humphrey and his subordinates in that programme. It is a sort of microcosm of life as you would imagine it in the FCO in London. The emphasis always being upon diplomacy and to not rocking the boat.

In fact a succinct description of that was cited by Lord Salisbury (a British Prime Minister at the turn of the nineteenth century): "English policy is to float downstream lazily, occasionally putting out the odd diplomatic boathook to avoid collisions". Beautifully put I always thought. "Government's policy, is usually to hope for no change in anything", quote Sir Humphrey.

The other one I always loved being when Sir Humphrey rebukes his secretary for cherishing minutes kept of meetings to record what happened " Minutes are not there to record facts Bernard, but to protect people". My final one on this was when the Permanent Secretary to the FCO protests "No one has ever accused the Foreign Office of patriotism". In response to a criticism that they were not helping their citizens abroad who found themselves in a fix.

Their peculiar technique is the art of talking without really saying anything, much in alignment with Sir Humphrey's inane chatter going on interminably and being utterly confusing. I think they must have courses for this.

Anyway enough, but it gives a general idea of the scene that prevailed then and actually for the most part life meandered along at a generally agreeable pace. Nobody upsetting anyone else apart from the odd disagreement or tiff. In any event and in the final analysis, it has to be kept in mind that the Governor is the emissary of the Queen, who has to exemplify tact and neutrality on all issues and to that end they serve her wonderfully. The general idea being to express no firm ideas upon anything!

Mark you and for the record, you are dealing with an ardent Royalist here. The pageant is wonderful and the Monarchy is a great foreign exchange earner in the U.K. with visiting tourists. Although ostensibly devoid of real power, the Queen enjoys a widespread adoration and respect and actually functions, I suspect, to keep our barmy politicians in check at times, given her attributes and sagacity. She certainly has her marbles so to speak, unlike some of them and is more popular with the public. In any case, would you really want the likes of Comrade Corbyn or, perhaps more aptly, Jean Claude Drunker on your postage stamps! Count me out on that one. More pertinently, she is still a big hit in the Dependent Territories, including the Islands.

March 1985 changed all that to some extent; well, so far as the FCO was concerned. Unfortunately the local Chief Minister and two of his cabinet ministers were arrested in a Ramada hotel in Miami as part of a sting operation set up by the U.S. authorities. It seemed to be in contravention of their racketeering laws and an alleged willingness to let the Islands remote runways be used for nocturnal flights and refueling purposes, assisting in the illicit importation of drugs into the U.S. The world media went berserk and there was full television coverage.

They had been secretly filmed in a hotel room allegedly

accepting monies to effect the illicit purpose. Now excuse me if I am wrong, but whatever the ostensible legality to entrapment, at least from a moral standpoint it is pretty obvious that someone encouraging the commitment of a crime surely is as culpable as the alleged offender they are targeting. Since if no enticement occurs then no crime will be committed.

Add this to it as well, from the actual film, I have never seen a more reluctant participant in taking the money than the Chief Minister and his colleagues. It was as if it was being forced upon them aggressively. It brought to mind a scene from California in the late sixties when flower power was the rage and everyone was wanting to get in on the act so to speak. It showed a tattooed, swarthy and hefty hells angel grabbing a passer by the collar and thrusting the then decapitated flowers into his chest and saying "Take de flowers or else". You take my meaning.

They were convicted and imprisoned. But it was the impact on the Islands that was also severe. People were shocked and the media had put it around that there were riots going on here. Guards were imported for the Governor's protection as it was thought that the U.K. side of things had been complicit in the matter. Actually Grand Turk just went deadly quiet as people recovered from the shock.

When a media delegation arrived unannounced they interviewed an old lady who, on being asked what she thought of the Chief Minister, meekly responded that he had been kind and was the Islands best tennis player. So much for turgid revolution. They were looking for a story and not the facts.

The FCO didn't handle it well either, because nothing had been put out by them and there was the customary silence on the issue, which always makes people suspect the worst. Nowadays they have publicity specialists to brand their image.

The main legacy from this was that mistrust had crept into the relationship between the locals and the U.K. Although in fairness to the FCO, their subsequent appointment of Governor, who incidentally stayed six years instead of the customary two, did try to pour calm on the much troubled waters and in fact largely succeeded. A much needed lesson in public relations for them.

Bringing the time line up to date, the U.K. displays an odd ambivalence towards the Islands. Strangely, under their E.U. commitments, they are anxious to impose every directive the E.U. want; although our relevance to them is baffling. Conversely on the subjects of policing and border control (which they have a legal responsibility for under the Island's Constitution) they display a mixture of parsimony (not wanting to spend a penny) and only feigned interest (although unwilling to do anything). As with any developing country crime correspondingly increases and immigration presents a very special problem for us.

In connection with the latter there is an old saying to the effect that if you simply sit in an open boat on the North Coast of Haiti and cast off, there is a five knot current which will bring you without any effort to guess where, Turks and Caicos!

Haiti is the economic disaster of the Western world. With unbelievable , poverty, corruption and instability. You cannot blame those poor souls for seeking a better life, and we have an illegal immigrant problem which is uncontrollable without assistance. We in fact have our own version of the Mediterranean crisis which Europe faces, but the U.K. will not incur any expense on the issue. Perhaps it is reflective of their E.U. notions of the importance of free movement! In those days we did not have problems of that magnitude.

Chapter 11

Our Revolutionary Registrar

You simply wouldn't have imagined that we had our own government employee who had the background of a revolutionary. Well so it was with Wilf Wickle. Our English Registrar of Companies. Well come to think of it and while we are about it, he was pretty much registrar of everything else as well; deaths and marriages, marriage officer, shipping registrar, patents, trademarks, coroner and so the list goes on. You name it he could do it. Wilf was a solicitor from the UK and in those days was in his forties. We always celebrated his birthday on New Year's day (must have been a tough one present wise with Christmas just past).

I describe Wilf as a revolutionary, but frankly he wasn't possessed of an adventurous spirit in the normal sense of the expression and he was certainly no Errol Flynn. He was tall, somewhat gangly, and if I had to stick an image to him he slightly resembled Beaker, the laboratory assistant out of the Muppets. I am not sure he had much in the way of family; a sister near Birmingham if memory serves correct and his alter mater there being Aston University. He was knowledgeable and congenial company.

He had largely forged his career with the government service in the Dependent Territories and had spent some years in Hong Kong. Thereafter he was posted to the Falkland Islands and that's where his narrative gets interesting. He was there when the Argies invaded in 1982 as Registrar of Companies. When the Governor there Rex whatever his name sensibly ordered surrender, as they were hopelessly outnumbered, the Governor found he had one unexpected dissident in his midst, namely Wilf.

Now Wilf was no Che Guevara or Pancho Villa, as he was reliability to the core and guaranteed usually to follow the protocol on anything. He occupied and barricaded himself inside the radio station there and encouragingly bleated out resistance to the occupation to the loyal islander population. In short, we had our own colonial version of Gandi propagating civil disobedience!

It had a peaceful ending, the Argies thinking they had a mad English nutter of Noel Coward vintage on their hands. They broke the siege without violence to Wilf and promptly shipped their erstwhile trouble maker off to Montevideo. Now that might have merited a George Cross award!

A short period after that Wilf ended up in the Islands. He lived on the Ridge with his adopted pet goat called Capra (Capricorn , earth sign, 1st January, by way of explanation). Wilf was a great believer in thrift and went everywhere on a moped, sporting a cap reminiscent of something out of Rommel's Afrika Corp. Being single, he must have saved a packet down the years given his frugal lifestyle.

As you can imagine he was extremely effective at his job and possessed common sense and initiative. A far cry from the legions of troglodytes you end up dealing with nowadays throughout the rest of the world, who can't do anything without a directive or manual to guide them (I must get away from this Orwell 1984 stuff).

Wilf's office was high up in a building on Front Street overlooking the sea. It was called Iron Building and with good reason. Only trouble was that it was severely rusting and pieces fell apart from the stairway seemingly every time you went up and down. It was almost on a par with Oswald and Leopold's office stairway. When you got to the office at the top you were in the Registry. Exceedingly dark with old rusted filing cabinets. But Wilf had a view from his big office window (actually it always seemed to be an open space) which was incomparable. You looked from high up over the beautiful azure waters of the sea onto the horizon. You could hypnotically gaze at it infinitely. How Wilf ever concentrated on his work I really do not know. It must have been the most picturesque office outlook on this planet.

His big pal on the Island was Bertie Windrush, the government legal draftsman. In some ways even more interesting that Wilf; he could have been straight out of the pages of an Evelyn Waugh or Somerset Maugham novel. A very eloquent barrister (or advocate as they are called) from Guernsey who spoke in a very witty dialogue, tongue in cheek so to speak.

His wife Maude was equally from the same thirties style era and reminded me a bit of Madame Arcarty in Blythe Spirit; delightfully eccentric. She looked and sounded a lot like Joyce Grenfell; that wonderfully English comedienne of bygone days. Everything fwightfully (she had a slight lisp) tickety boo as it were . Although a somewhat diminutive lady (she could scarcely be five feet), it stuck in my mind that she appeared to have enormous feet; the appearance accentuated by her tendency to wear extra large sandals all the time. Curiously enough I later found out that she was a qualified chiropodist.

They were magnificent hosts and we spent many a Sunday lunch at their place up on the ridge, listening to Bertie's recounting of amusing anecdotes. Bertie reminded me a lot, both to look at and listen to, of Peter Tomlinson who played the slightly pompous father in Mary Poppins.

When he set up practice as a newly qualified advocate (lawyer) in Guernsey, whenever he heard a knocking at the door of presumably prospective clients he rather hoped they would go away and leave him in peace and would not answer the door! He would have done as well to have a door mat inscribed with "buzz off" on it instead of "welcome". Not the most commercially ambitious of lawyers as you can see. In fact he had a considerable intellect with a forte for writing research books on famous families; the De Havillands being the subject he was writing about at that time (as I recall the famous aviation company and the actress who is still with us).

He was actually a capable draftsman with an ability to express himself succinctly and without ambiguity; something today's scriveners tend to sorely lack. He wasn't verbose in his language either.

Today we are simply deluged with endless laws and regulations emanating from Europe, Brussels and Strasbourg, created by unelected bureaucrats. In fact the recent Brexit caused me to realize something extraordinary. Many of those laws are neither debated or even read by our elected Members of Parliament in the U.K., but just rubber stamped through. Although the Islands are not part of the E.U. we suffer the same fate here; as the FCO are compelled to impose them and I don't think anyone is either aware of or bothered by this. You suddenly realize that the U.K. lost its own sovereignty decades ago. We were all asleep at the wheel so to speak, with the exception of the bureaucrats and politicians with vested interests in this calamity. I know, get back on track.

Bertie worked in the Attorney General's Chambers downtown and there was an amusing rivalry that went on between the characters that occupied it. Of course there was Bertie, but along side him the Attorney General himself, Duncan Cockalot and Crown Counsel Horace Fastaway. There was a certain stridency or inherent contrast in personalities. Horace was a down to earth get on with it type. But Duncan was an effervescent personality, extremely bright, slightly eccentric, and wait for it (what drove Bertie mad) excessively busying himself all the time with enthusiastic theories on everything, like an over exuberant schoolboy. By contrast Bertie was drily laconic and could not for the life of him understand the need for fussing all the time.

When Duncan deservedly got his Queens Counsel elevation (bear in mind it's called taking silk) and was romping proudly down the corridors in his robes, Bertie typically couldn't resist the comment "the rustle of silk is positively deafening in this place". Pure Wodehouse material. Actually there was no animosity between them, which was the important thing. Duncan was forever in his own world and his antics were a source for Bertie's dry sardonic sense of humour. A far cry perhaps from the Inner Temple in London.

Those were very different days indeed. Today there seems to be an ardent desire to litigate over anything, even when there is little cause to do so and of course lawyers are essentially guns for hire. I will always remember what a an old sagacial litigation lawyer once imparted to me. "Only sue for money, never for injured pride or on account of seeking legal address, only the lawyers are guaranteed to make money." As if to reinforce this notion there was a famous wine bar just outside the Inner

Temple in London on the Strand. It was called the "Wig and Pen Club" and of course it was frequently full of eccentric legal characters with many a witty anecdote to tell. I remember that they had a print of a famous Hogarth cartoon on one wall (he was a famous 18th century illustrator). It depicted a cow. Its head being pulled by a plaintiff and its tail by the defendant in the action over its ownership. Meanwhile sitting on a stool and furiously milking its udders productively into a bucket was the lawyer!

As to the corollary to these characters lives: Wilf subsequently went back to the U.K. setting up a small legal practice on the south Devonshire coast. I actually visited him there, but in the early nineties life was already becoming difficult economically for small provincial firms. He had taken his Dominican maid with him whom he married and then relocated in retirement to the Dominican Republic

Due to a municipal muck up he managed to get free electricity for over two years where he lived there; which ranked something of an achievement in his somewhat parsimonious scale of things. He still lives there happily married with a family (I have a feeling that Capra the goat stayed put in Grand Turk).

Duncan went in the opposite direction to Wilf and ended up as Attorney General in the Falkland Islands; where he was well regarded and retired there. One could well see him presiding over sheep grazing disputes.

Bertie retired to Guernsey and again I was fortunate to visit him and Maude there. Sadly he had a recurrence of the cancer which had troubled him before he came to the Islands and he died in 1987. Again all unforgettable characters.

Chapter 12

Specimens And Legal Bovver

Following the political upheaval resulting from the arrests in Miami it was generally feared that the widespread adverse publicity would have a detrimental affect on the economy for the Islands. Things certainly went very quiet. So we resolved to back our horses both ways as it were and apply for immigration status in British Columbia Canada; through my wife's aunt who had status there. It was a bit of insurance just in case. A return to London, although not out of the question, entailed as it were somewhat of a tail between the legs syndrome, which frankly neither of us were keen upon.

Apart from the plethora of forms that needed completion there was the necessity to have a medical exam locally by an approved physician. Enter Dr. Balouchee onto the scene. We duly rang his surgery to make the appointment with a very polite lady, his wife as it turned out, and in turn received copious instructions how to reach the surgery. The latter may seem a bit far fetched as it couldn't have been more than half a mile away.

It entailed a walk down Front Street along the low sea wall and then on into a hinterland of buildings that ensued. It was surprising how many nooks and crannies made up this area of town, Eventually we went down an alley way and into what seemed a backyard and in front of us stood a grey wooden building; a bit like the domestic dwelling in "Little House on the Prairie". Very neat with squared windows but with the exception of an enormously pointed roof, which seemed cavernous.

Only instead of the vast wheat fields of the U.S. prairies we were in a yard surrounded by chickens scuttling around and a goat with its head in an overturned trash can looking for scraps. There was a grey painted front door and to its right a brass plate with the inscription "Dr. John Balouchee M.B.S.". We knocked and went in.

Everything inside looked grey as well, as if one gigantic vat of paint, on special sale, had done the whole building inside and out. We were greeted by a charming petite lady, Mrs. Balouchee, who ushered us to a settee set against a wall, temporarily dislodging a very furry cat who evidently took umbridge at this. "He won't be long" indicating to the surgery door which was slightly ajar, through which bellowed "now Mary none of that, we all know I'm not busy, so show them in."

I had been expecting something along latin lines given his obviously Italian sounding name, but that was in his ancestry as it turned out. He was English through and through. Probably in his late fifties, medium to heavy build, straight combed back hair, a high forehead, heavy glasses through which twinkled the sort of eyes that enjoyed a good joke. He wore a shirt and tie and a sports jacket and with a stethoscope around his neck that would could have been a relic from the Science Museum. He actually wore corduroy trousers, in fact very comfortable even in our tropical climate. He positively wreaked of comfort and affability. He read the forms and muttered "easily done", "easily done". The examinations were quick and trouble free.

Then Mary brought a tray of tea and biscuits into the surgery, left and we chatted for some time. It's always fascinating to find out how people end up in the Islands and Dr. Balouchee was no exception. He had qualified in London and held a senior position in one of the leading hospitals there. He had then travelled to Africa and became Chief Medical Office to the entire country of Cameroon. Then after some years left and fulfilled the same position in Saskatchewan in Canada. After a further period of years he visited the Islands to do a report of some medical nature and met his wife, from South Caicos, and thereafter decided to eke out the latter part of his career as a general practitioner in Grand Turk. He emphatically imparted to us that the Islands were the healthiest place on earth and he was so happy there he never intended to depart.

Like all people who are truly interesting he asked questions and was intrigued by our own background. It was one of those conversations you could have delightfully prolonged. Upon getting up to leave I suddenly remembered something, "don't you have to send specimens to Canada for examination?" He pawed the air in a dismissive fashion and with a smile said "don't worry, I always send them a dog dropping and it never seems to bother them."

Returning, as so often happened walking either way down Front Street, you would bump into Peanuts; an institution in the Islands, nearly always by the Post Office. Let me explain. We have a specialty dish in the Islands called conch. It is a mollusc which is derived from a beautiful pinkish shell (they are sought after by tourists) and it has a taste not easy to compare with other seafood. To my mind it is delicious and is dealt up in a myriad of different ways. Conch salad with lime juice, conch chowder being a soup and one of my favourites being conch fritters (fried in batter). The latter was Peanuts particular offering and they were simply divine to eat. She had a wheel cart from which these delicacies ushered forth.

Peanuts heralded I think from Grand Turk (the nickname I was never entirely sure of) and she must have been in her seventies then. Always jovial. She was a small rotund lady and her fritters were renowned everywhere. In fact the conch shell even features in our flag; in the shield along with the Turks Head cactus and lobster (for a long time I mistook the latter for a mosquito, from the way it is depicted, and I was sharply rebuked for my error).

After succumbing to temptation and consuming some delicious fritters we had a letter to post. The Post Office had to be one of the oldest buildings in Grand Turk. It had very large green doors as an entrance; perhaps eight feet high and a breadth of six feet . It was always padlocked at night but someone lost the key on one occasion. So the next day, and until it could be opened, customers simply ingressed and egressed by stepping over the large window sills on either side of the doors (as the windows never seemed to be locked).

There were p.o. boxes outside but many had long since rusted to the point where they could no longer be opened and anyway it was so much nicer to go in and speak to the friendly staff who would hand you your mail.

As we were just about reaching our office we bumped into Ernie. His offices were a couple of doors along from our own, fronting on the beach. He was slinging some enormous plastic bags of goodness knows what into the back of his car; probably shredded paper.

Now Ernie Pickles was not the sort of person you wanted to end up on the wrong side of. To begin with he stood about six foot four inches tall and was built something along the lines of the Forth Rail Bridge. He also had some obscure martial arts special ty called Tae Kwon Do something or other to his credit; which probably meant he could kill just by looking at you. He was the sort of character who could hand you your body back with the limbs knotted.

My wife, delightfully lacking in tact and obviously in a mischievous mood on this occasion, shouted out "hello Ernie, doing a bit of banking". For a moment I wondered which one of my neck vertebrae was about to get snapped. But he stopped hand on hips and chuckled with laughter. That was Ernie, if (and a big one at that) he liked you. For some reason Ernie also liked to lapse into a sort of colloquial, gruff, deep cockney when he spoke. The common touch if you like.

Now the flip side, and in fact the real Ernie. He was from public school in the UK (private, expensive to our North American friends), from a professional family. Went to one of the best universities there and qualified as a solicitor (lawyer). He had also been a member of one of the most prestigious law practices in the City of London. A highly able lawyer and woe betide any over confident adversary who under rated him in that regard; they did so at their peril. He had a very astute eye for the law and well honed commercial instincts. I subsequently got on like a house on fire with him and liked his company.

When he wanted he could speak eloquently and be a toasting masters dream. But in colloquial dialect (West Road, in Grand Turks as he liked to put it), well, you needed a Berlitz translation to make him out. A real chameleon but a good card to boot as they say. He also had very esteemed contacts and friends back in the U.K. In some ways Ernie (being somewhat thin on top) was the only Bovver Boy/Skinhead solicitor I had ever come across.

Ernie was one to put his money where his mouth was. He invested in Grand Turk in car dealerships and real estate which gave employment. That was very tricky in those days in what was to say the least a fledgling economy. Few had the courage to do that. His employees invariably had nicknames, as did all of us, and collectively he would call them his 'dog crew'. Ernie called himself 'the Gasman', as he had developed a successful gas supply business. Which was in considerable demand; especially for cooking and barbeques. True to his nature he believed in service and he could have been our very own 'Ernie the fastest gasman in the West' (alright, enough of the Benny Hill).

Fittingly he had an expression which I never forgot, it came from the Godfather, "keep your friends close, but your enemies closer". Thankfully I never ranked in the latter category. I heard once that some rather unctuous little weasel happened to make an opprobrious remark aimed at Ernie in a bar. Ernie simply turned around, grabbed him by the lapels, lifted him up to his eye level (the unfortunate miscreant being about two foot off the ground) looking like Tom the Cat being grabbed by Butch the Bulldog in Tom and Jerry. Roaring at him "war you mean": and then dropping him, without the benefit of the parachute. Point made and taken.

A few months later we took a trip to the Dominican Republic; our first holiday from Grand Turk. We were on the same flight to Puerta Plata there as Ernie and since he was "visitin family in Santo Domingo" which was where we were going, we shared a rental car. We had a great time, but in assessing the mileage to the gallon, I think the number of Presidente beers consumed en route would have been the appropriate marque.

As it turned out we never needed our insurance, so we did not pursue Canadian residency, but I truly enjoyed our reconnoiter with our local G.P.

Chapter 13

Of Fireworks And Commissions

It would be no exaggeration to say that the Islands welcomed in the New Year of 1986 with a bang and not with a whimper. We had the biggest firework of all. Our Philatelic Bureau was set alight. A very old wooden building which housed our historic collection of stamps going back many years. Our stamps are notable and it is another reason why people know of the Islands as philatelists . I remember seeing one when I was about eight, showing a salt raker in one of the Island's water pans, and thinking where on earth could that exotic place be; little realizing one day I would end up living there.

We were at a New Year's Eve party at the time, a fancy dress one as I recall (I went as a white rabbit) and suddenly gazing out of the window I saw a colossal surge of orange flame about a mile away across the bay of the Island. The Bureau being well beyond Front Street and actually not far from Dr. Balouchee's surgery.

We drove over to see. The sight of a white rabbit alighting from the Green Goddess Cadillac must have had an alarming effect upon some bystanders. I remember one slurry spoken reveller saying "I gotta give this stuff up" rubbing his eyes and not believing what he saw. To that extent I may have for once helped the tea total movement. Doubt it though. The Building was completely destroyed and thankfully the adjoining premises were just slightly singed.

Those premises belonging to Percy DeBlakeney, a well respected lawyer. Percy merits description. He was a very distinguished practitioner acting for important personages. He was polished, having been to Eton (the English public school); unlike Ernie's efforts to sound like someone from E.10 (in the East End of London). I think he even had aristocracy in his lineage and could also add Cambridge and Sandhurst Military establishment to his curriculum vitae. As you might expect, he was very well groomed and turned out. Invariably courteous and professional in his dealings and he brought a certain exactitude to his work. So much so that if I recall correctly he even stipulated "Anno Domini" when dating his corporate documents; demonstrating a succinct focus on the history. He was rumoured to be of the buddist faith, which would tend to indicate a philosophic faculty to add to his other considerable intellectual attributes. He was the embodiment of class; the hallmark on the silver if you like. A tremendous advertisement for the Islands and also I am straying off the point again.

The fire set in train a motion of events which were to have monumental consequences for the Islands. By the way, I should add that no one was either killed or injured in the fire thankfully; we tend not to hurt people in our disasters if we can help it. It was rumoured and alleged that the fire had been initiated as a form of political protest involving a political figure and the powers that be, the FCO in London, were intent on holding a commission of enquiry to get to the bottom of it.

It also has to be said that at that time relations between the local government and the FCO had become somewhat strained and the allegation that there had been rife corruption in the Public Works Department of Government served as a further catalyst to what followed. Enter on stage Bijou Flem-Grouper QC. An eminent U.K. lawyer specializing in public administration law and the duly appointed Commissioner. Bijou was one of those larger than life characters, pleasant, with heavy side burns and to look at could have passed as a portly uncle out of a Jane Austen novel.

We were actually to get three Commissions in all over the ensuing years and from the locals perspective I think the overall reaction was one of pure bafflement. Supporting staff were brought in and premises set up for what was to follow. It never fails to surprise and to amuse me how when these sort of things happen there are suddenly no end of supporting characters in the cast ready to jump on the bandwagon.

We suffer from a plethora of it nowadays, with experts and consultants whenever a government project arises or an expert assessment is deemed necessary. Quite simply they are all feeding out of the publicly funded trough and as a consequence they do not have the same accountability that you might get in a private organization. Although sometimes nowadays you wonder at that as well.

Our Chief Minister at the time was a benign old soul nicknamed "BOPS". Very much revered by the locals for kindnesses he had dealt out down the years. I am not going into the intricacies of the Commissions. The first, was held into the fire at the Philatelic Bureau, Bascombe House as it was called, and the corruption allegations produced an outcome which from the FCO's perspective merited a suspension of the Constitution. With the result that a UK controlled interim government was formed presided over by the Governor with a council of four esteemed locals. The British also brought in select personnel. It lasted for two years.

The irony being that once further elections were held immediately thereafter the populace promptly returned to office the politico accused of being at the heart of the fire. He had been held by the enquiry to be unfit to hold public office. So much for all the judicial shenanigans and expense. Actually he was a likeable fellow and I am still not sure that the allegations were proven at all and he certainly strenuously denied them.

The second Commission a few months later served as a comeuppance for the lawyer Jasper Stoneyheart. The Governor's Office, tired of its legal entanglements with him, chose a commission, because it really served to alter the ground rules and widen the goalposts of the issue. That Commission found that he had engaged in a conflict of interests in setting up privately and he was consequently booted off the Island.

The third Commission at the end of it all served to pave a future for the Islands development. What you have to bear in mind about these Commissions, and particularly in that latter case, is that the FCO is not bound by the findings and that they often elect to adopt courses of action falling into line with their own particular agenda.

As so often happens in life, the events of one set of circumstances very often spawn interesting developments in another, and so it proved to be the case with the Commissions. The U.S. authorities at that time were wanting to extradite a local for questioning in connection with some matter and as the Commission lawyers were in town it seemed fortuitous for them to instruct one of their number to represent their case before our courts. Tommy Coster was the counsel chosen for this purpose, in effect he was Bijou Flem-Grouper's right hand man. Very personable and polite but clearly with a flare for advocacy which explained his presence.The sitting judge at that time was Horace Yardarm, and he was to preside over the case to be heard. Horace was a pink and ruddy complexioned man, in his early sixties, sporting a permanent smile. He was small of stature and very popular amongst the legal fraternity. Nothing was so serious that it couldn't be amicably dealt with over a gin and tonic (or preferably several). I think this was his last case.

The defense to the action was to be handled by Arty Grocer QC. He had been specially brought in from Europe for the case. Much to the chagrin of Tommy, Arty and Horace seemed to know each other and there followed a preamble before the case started something along the lines of "How is Mrs. Betty Grocer " from Horace and a reciprocal greeting from Arty. It must have seemed like two long separated freemasons reuniting their friendship again. Objectivity seemingly having flown out the window. In fact Tommy must have felt positively out of the whole business.

It could only get worse, and so it did. Extradition is a specialist subject as it turned out and back then there was little in the way of authorative written guidance for Horace upon the subject matter in hand. However he delighted in imparting to the court that he had just received from his clerk the specialist book on the subject and that would serve as his guide. A somewhat coy smile came over Arty's face as Horace looked at him. Then Horace , having looked at the jacket cover to the book, beamed and said "why Arty the book is written by you". "Yes M'Lud, I believe it is" he retorted. As to what followed: Game set and match to the defence. Tommy was crest fallen.

The gravy on the dish was yet to be served up. Tumultuous

rejoicing came from outside the courthouse and music started when the verdict was handed down and announced. The local lad was safe from the rapacious grips of Uncle Sam. When Tommy walked outside there was dancing and a large lady gyrated up to him and wiggled against Tommy in celebration . He simply smiled and left.

There was some consolation in all this. Tommy found himself invited to dinner, along with ourselves, to Wilf's, our Registrar of everything, up at his home on the Ridge. The meal and overall hospitality was justifiably entrusted to his maid, Mariah, who served delicious Dominican cuisine and provided exemplary service constantly. It was like Manuel in Fawlty Towers constantly filling the guests wine glasses almost each time you took a sip, but without the disastrous spilling consequences.

She was a happy bubbly lady, rounded and scarcely four feet six inches tall. The amazing backdrop to the evening was the relationship between her and Wilf. Obviously cordial and affectionate, but rather like the memsahib and his punkahwallah. Every time anything was to be done Wilf raised and clapped his hands and Mariah jerked into action. It was comical; but the equal rights lobby today would be having kittens if they witnessed it. In fact Tommy commented laughingly that they were exactly like husband and wife. A truism as it turned out.

Chapter 14

Beachcoming And Bar Repartee

The beach, just across the road from the old Salt Raker Inn, had a very special charm of its own. For one thing there was hardly any sound at all save for the gentle lapping of the waves at the shoreline, with an occasional mild cascading of the surf. The sea was azure blue during the day and twinkled silver as dusk approached. In fact for that part of town it was unique, as Front Street and the houses along Duke Street just had rocky shoreline for the most part.

About half a mile offshore the depth of the sea suddenly plunged from about thirty feet to some eight thousand. This was the Turks Island Passage, a famous thorough fare for ships down the ages and extended about twenty miles west to the Island of South Caicos, which was the start of the Caicos Archipelago. That in turn arched some forty miles further west and eventually reaches Providenciales and West Caicos.

The drop just mentioned is called the Wall and it offers some of the best diving in the world. It is Grand Turk's primary source of tourism and the likes of Jacques Cousteau and other notables have visited it several times. South Caicos was where the world record had been set for the deepest unassisted free dive; without air tanks or any other breathing aid.

The Salt Raker Inn itself had a delightful charm being some one hundred and fifty years old. It's very reminiscent of the sort of quaint houses you find in the Florida Cays often standing solitary. A typical Hemingway type of retreat.

Fronting the road it has a white interspersed fence with brilliant showers of bright red bougainvilla pouring and cascading over it. A small garden behind and then latticed windows serving as the offices for the Inn, whilst above stood a balcony with hotel rooms which although somewhat archaic had the finest views over the road, the sea and the horizon.

To idle away hours sitting on a rocking chair on that balcony reading or just day dreaming in the balmy breeze was sheer bliss, an elixir from heaven, with a rum punch to hand to perfect the experience. Time was simply of no consequence. And the guests, be they tourists or people on government business, simply loved the place.

The beach was a sort of common denominator of sorts and sooner or later you would meet just about any visitor to the Island taking a dip. In fact it was not unusual to spark up acquaintances by treading water and chatting. As a resident you became an immediate source of curiosity to those wanting to know about the place. Especially as the beach was quite small just there, probably no more than about a hundred feet wide. The important thing being that it was down town (the much larger beach being to the south and fronting the Governor's residence which lay about a mile or so further on).

The beach had hosted a variety of characters in its time. A few years previously a businessman passing through the Islands so to speak had, at the request of the Authorities in London, been detained by the police here. They wanted to send

Chapter 14

someone out from London to question him. The only place to house him, given the circumstances, was the prison. As you can imagine our prison was old; it could have been twinned with the Alamo in Texas (after the siege!).

The official duly arrived after a few days to question him. He went to the prison and upon asking the warden to see him was told " Sorry he's not in". Flabberghasted the official asked where he was. "You'll find him on the beach, he's not going anywhere." Lo and behold the official found him on our beach, sitting on a towel lent to him by the warden, reading a newspaper to the accompaniment of a bottle of beer and a cigarette. The interview was duly concluded there and then and the fellow was found free to go his way as obviously he was no threat to law and order. Casual incarceration you might call it.

Now at the other end of the spectrum of beach visitors came our very own new Chief Justice, Walter Winthrop. Walter was a tall man. At first impression he rather resembled the bus inspector, Blakey, in the British comedy 'On the Buses'. But Walter certainly lacked any vacant expression to his countenance. He had sharp keen intelligent eyes. Although British he had been brought up in Zimbabwe and had rapidly moved up the legal ladder there, then in London, ending up as a Chancery barrister (usually the domain of the brightest lawyers).

Retiring as a judge this current appointment was something in the line of a sinecure for him and he periodically came out to hear cases. Whereas his predecessor, Horace, had a somewhat laissez-faire attitude towards time, Walter was the exact antithesis. He was renowned for dispatching his case load with celerity so he could head for the beach. Not to suggest that he overlooked anything; in fact he had a mind like a laser. It was rumoured that he often wore his swimming trunks under his

97

judges robes. You could imagine his towel draped under his gavel on the bench, with Salt Raker Inn inscribed on it.

Once a somewhat garrulous and long winded attorney addressed the court "and now , if I might get to the very point of the issue", and Walter drily piped in "indeed sir, I wish you would". You see what I mean. Actually he was the soul of courtesy, he was just possessed of that type of humour. You often saw him hastily heading for the beach in his trunks, towel slung across his shoulder, whilst attorneys were still seen behind him pontificating outside the court following the closure of the session. I liked him a lot and he had a humane, sagacial quality to him not always evident in today's world.

He used to like to come to our office, just across the road from the beach, and have a cup of tea and a chat. He had actually quit Zimbabwe (Southern Rhodesia as it then was) back in 1965, when the white minority claimed UDI (Unilateral Declaration of Independence) but had a very profound knowledge of how colonial territories operated. This was not a guy to pull his punches on any issue and he was not overcome with political correctness (two words which were an anomaly in those days, but an all too prevalent feature of life today).

He was particularly critical at what he saw as the seeming insensitivity and sclerotic behavior of the FCO and the way it had handled the recent crises in the Islands. After all how could you run a country from a desk four and a half thousand miles away in accordance with a set of bureaucratic standards that had its roots firmly set in the nineteenth century. As far as he could discern the Governor was a mere cypher of Whitehall in London and functioned in a reporting back puppet type role, rather than involving himself meaningfully in the affairs of the Islands.

Things haven't changed by the way, just more bureaucracy

and interference from the EU and OECD (international organizations, staffed to the gunnels with bureaucrats which boss the FCO, who willingly submit and in turn coerce the Islands; not elected mind, but technocrats with tenure seemingly for life). Wow, but these were certainly revelations then and it showed the sort of perspicuity this fellow had. Obdurate (stubborn) and obfuscation (obscure) were other adjectives he used frequently when the FCO came up in conversation, but I think enough of that for now.

I saw him until the end of 1986. Strangely enough I was in London about five years later; in Chancery Lane at the heart of the legal district. I was in a telephone box, making an unavoidably long call, when he passed by walking briskly; looking immaculate in his dark suit, waistcoat, umbrella and even a bowler hat. My previous memory of him having been in his swimming trunks or judicial robes. I wanted to end the call and pursue him but couldn't. Once off the phone I looked for him in vain. Sadly that was the very last I did see of Walter.

By now you will have correctly concluded that the narrator of this story has created the impression that the Islands were jammed packed full of offbeat legal loons and little else. There were certainly a few, but time to digress as in truth there were many more interesting characters outside of that fraternity.

In any case lawyers tend to be a vain breed and always err towards talking about themselves or their occupation. And no better place to digress than to the bar of the Salt Raker Inn, located at the rear of the premises at the end of a beautiful garden, covered in bougainvilla, and hibiscus where guests and customers ate at fairly rickety tables on collapsible chairs. The food was great though, especially if you liked lobster and conch. Now there were lawyers usually there (I know, stop it) but it also had a clientele of other very colourful sorts.

My landlady was one such. Ruby Roublehoff. Ruby was Canadian and her father had made an absolute bundle dealing on the Edmonton Stock Exchange there. When he died his fortune was divided between Ruby and her three sisters and hence her justification to live life to the full by coming to the Turks and Caicos Islands, which enjoyed a tax free status and an easy life style. I got on well with her. She was of pleasing appearance and there was something definitely of the out of doors about her.

She stood about five foot five tall, perhaps a little plump, and seemed to shun make up without any ill effect to her appearance. Her hair was tightly tied back into a pony tail and she had golden earrings the size of hula hoops (alright, not quite, but big). Add to that she usually wore white trousers and a blue and white laterally striped tea shirt for much of the time. There was something of Tug Boat Annie about her, which was fitting because along with her partner she simply adored the boating life and lived on them whenever possible. Her partner, Mitch, who must have been about twenty years her junior (she would have been in her mid-fifties to guess) was adept at boat mechanics and especially engines and was a very easy pleasant going type of guy.

Although they had accommodation in the same complex as ours (she owned the whole place) they did spend a lot of time living on their boat moored up in North Creek; just below and west of the Ridge. Being of practical persuasion they paired life down to its simplicities and were not ones for any sort of waste. Even their dinner plates and cutlery were made of extreme tensile strength biscuit, so they could eat them up at the end of any meal. Great thinking I always thought, even if not quite for me.

She also had something of a gypsy look to her and I could

imagine her doing horoscope readings in a striped tent gazing into a crystal ball. Perhaps with boozy Monty as a customer and saying to him "you like drink" (you could smell it before he even turned the corner) Monty wandering off afterwards muttering to himself "amazing how they do it". Just an impression mind you.

Ruby and Mitch had a cockatoo parrot called "Birdie". Where he picked up his language from heavens knows, but you often heard him cackling obscenities in the backyard. There used to be a little visiting dog called Mike and the bird drove him crazy, cackling "Mike", " Mike" and causing the little fellow to run around desperately seeking the source of his name at the behest of this evil notioned parrot. Birdie could be dangerous as well if you didn't value your fingers. His line being "Scratch Birdie" and then delivering a savage nip to the unsuspecting victim who happened to fall for it.

I was scrolling through one of Alfie's historical journals one evening and fascinatingly came across a piece he had done on Mary Reid and Anne Bonney. Believe it or not these were lady pirate captains who ran their ships around Pine Cay, to the West of the Islands (much sought after for its fresh water lens there) in the seventeenth century, but having male crews. So we had equal opportunity even in those days. Mary Reid in particular was depicted wearing a blue and white a striped shirt, white trousers and gold earrings. I know, say no more. Reincarnation happens.

Ruby was helpful and upon taking up occupation of our offices and living accommodation it was quickly realized that the existing bed would not do. It had actually fallen apart. So she lent us an inflatable airbed from off the boat, until the new bed ordered from Miami arrived. Slight problem was it had a leak.

So that at night you virtually collapsed with giddiness upon blowing the massive thing up to a slumbent level. By morning it had deflated to a point where you were almost lying on hard ground. The timing worked out though. Because by that time it had reached an unsleepable level and it was pretty much time to get up. Also Frankie, our adopted donkey so to speak, was braying out at the front gate for his morning ration of carrots.

Despite being a far cry from the luxury of London, I really liked those premises. They were somehow homely. The accommodation at the rear was simple and cozy. Towards the front there was a large wooden partition with a door leading to the office. Off to the left was the consulting room with large desk. It was cavernous and had immense windows front and rear. A large banana plant stood outside the front garden area.

The main office was about forty feet long by fifteen feet wide, leading to the front door and either side large louvred windows. All along the side walls there were windows with venetian blinds, so the lighting factor was always good. When you opened the front door in the morning, you were looking at the beach and sea across the road and the wonderful sound of the surf. I really could not better that scenario anywhere.

In those days you didn't even have fax in the Islands, in fact it was something of a new innovation in London then. Telephones were there of course, but our main communication device for what was international work was a telex machine. Now gone altogether, but the banks still use them I am told. The latter was essentially a loud ticker tape machine.

Now given the time zone difference (much work coming from Europe then) this gadget could suddenly and loudly come to life at any time during the night. It was a source of much excitement because it usually signified work coming in, so you didn't mind being woken up. It was momentous anticipation.

You could understand how people felt when anxious news was awaited. Somehow distance made it more intriguing, but the next day entailed a shorter distance but no less exciting a prospect. A visit to Salt Cay.

Chapter 15

Musings At The Airport

For the record, Salt Cay was always my favourite Island. It lies about ten miles due south of Grand Turk and is clearly visible from its southernmost tip, with just the small uninhabited islet of Cotton Cay (actually owned by the Discardi Brothers), lying a shade closer to the east south east. It's perhaps surprisingly not much less than the size of Grand Turk and is a sort of flat triangle in shape. You fly there, as the provision boat went only twice weekly in those days. So it was off to the airport. The Green Goddess was to be left in the car park, to share with donkeys and cattle for the two nights we were to be there.

Getting out of the car we were ambushed by the wonderful aroma of baking. You felt like the Bisto Kid, following the scented trail. The source was a little building set apart from the airport and run by a local guy, Ossie 'Dough Dough' Wimborne. He had been the baker and chef at the old Pan Am tracking station, which closed about two years previously and he had gained a small concession to set up at the airport. Ossie was a cheerful character and he originally came from Jamaica. He must have stood about six foot five. Actually he was a Rasta and had long locks, which for cooking hygiene reasons had to be either cut or accommodated under a hat.

Somehow he had procured an elongated chefs hat which stood about four foot tall to encase his locks. Luckily or perhaps by design he had chosen a bakery with cathedral type ceilings so that his potential standing of ten feet five could be coped with. I never saw him going in or out but reason dictates that he either took the hat off or propelled himself laterally through the door.

His bakery and its temptations were beyond resistance. His particular speciality were trays of bread and butter pudding; with cinnamon, sultanas and a gooey substance I know not what which was simply divine. He also did the best bread I had ever tasted along with a host of different pastries. It was a weightwatchers nemesis and a nightmare for any dietician. By the way, why is it the latter presumably health fanatics always seem to look anorexic and with blemished skin, in short ill. Probably the worry; they all seem to be neurotic. I once told one I met in the Islands that I wasn't keen on lettuce and she looked at me with hatred as if I had just blasphemed the patron saint of dull food.

Well that was breakfast taken care of and armed with our brown bags of goodies we went into the airport for coffee and our check in. Time, as you can guess then, was a fairly flexible concern and flights were to an approximation. Our pilot was sitting along side us having a coffee in the departure lounge, Max Mightmakeit, a Canadian.

He and his family had come to the Islands for what turned out to be a one year layoff, along with a batch of other Canadian pilots. They had been temporarily let go by Pacific Western, the west coast carrier, due to the economic situation then. The local airline had readily employed them as there was a shortage of pilots. The too few local pilots that we had were excellent, there just weren't enough of them at that time.

Their living conditions weren't the most salubrious. They were essentially holed up in the old naval base, which had been abandoned at the northern most tip of the Island. There were living quarters and when the U.S. handed the base over to the Islands Government they were in superb condition; which was the way with the U.S. Government; always supporting their service personnel, up to the hilt in those days. Unfortunately once vacant, most of the apartments and facilities were in effect cannibalized; with basins, toilets and other essentials having been ripped out and carted off by opportunistic scavengers. Some were still inhabitable and that's where they were accommodated.

Max was very conscientious and was forever studying and revising his manuals for his recall to Canada; which happily happened for all of them after the one year stint in the Islands was over and deregulation of the airlines had occurred in Canada. However they took great memories with them when they left. They were all a great bunch to be with, but were a little slow to appreciate the more casual regime which existed down here then. There were two particular situations which he recounted.

Firstly, on one occasion he found that not only had he been given clearance to land but that another colleague had also been given clearance by the tower. Trouble being that they were approaching the same runway from different directions at the same time. Thankfully it wasn't that close an encounter and both pilots followed the well accepted procedure of banking to their respective right to ensure missing one another. Once on the ground both pilots lambasted the official in charge; actually blowing a gasket would be the more correct description. The official, totally unphased saying 'there's a technical expression for this type of situation' to which both pilots screamed ' yes, bloody negligence'. It made not one iota of an impact.

In the second incident Max and the other pilots were curious that every time they checked with the control tower what the temperature was they got the same answer, '72 degrees'; be it night, daytime whatever. It seemed impossible. Apparently this is crucial information, as temperature affects the performance of the aircraft.

Approaching the airport one afternoon Max had radioed yet again asking the temperature and he got the same answer. He asked the controller to check the barometer/thermometer whatever. The answer came back 'it seems to be stuck', it had in fact been broken for at least six months. Thinking this appeased Max the controller radioed the customary "Turkey Tower out" to which Max responded "you certainly are".

Now no musings about the Airport would be complete without a mention of Fleety Skiwiffs. Fleety was best described as a frustrated aviator as to fly was his one ambition in life. Resident in Grand Turk he had a pal, Basil Bungy-Phipps, also a resident but who could fly and most importantly had his own plane and on the odd occasion gave lessons to Fleety. On one particular occasion, Basil being off Island, Fleety borrowed the plane and took it for a whirl so to speak. How this skipped the attentions of the Airport officials is beyond belief.

His problem came when attempting to land as for some reason he didn't realize the undercarriage wasn't down. In fact he made several attempts at landing and the propellers actually scraped the runway, whereupon he pulled up and aborted, being heard on the radio saying "whoops, try that one again" each time. How a serious accident didn't result was anyone's guess. He eventually was able to land and he duly made reparations for the slightly buckled propellers to a furious Basil when he got back on Island.

Our intrepid aviator subsequently went to Florida, got properly licensed and bought a plane of his own. Of course he decided to fly it down to the Islands on his own from there. Prudence was never his strong point. It was a small aircraft and he would have to hop down getting refuelled en route. Problem being that he hadn't fully checked the weather and hadn't reckoned on a surfeit of cloud during the course of his flight. He didn't have an instrument rating and had to manage by flying on pure 'dead reckoning" as they call it, i.e. solely by what you can see.

Some way down the Bahamian chain of islands he realized he was running short of fuel and because of the cloud cover, he simply didn't know where he was. Suddenly he spotted a hole in the clouds and to use his own expression he "went for it". Luckily it turned out to be Long Island, with an air strip and where he could refuel.

His problems weren't over yet. On taking off again and eventually reaching Grand Turk, it was growing dark. Not having filed a flight plan and since they were not expecting him, the runway lights were turned off as the airport had closed! He made an intuitive guess at his position and that of the runway and, the patron saint of silly asses being on his side, he got down safely. Couldn't resist that one. And wait for it, amazing as it may seem, he is still alive and well today!

Not the ideal topics of conversation just before a flight, so I will move on.

The planes the local airline used were called Britten-Norman Islanders and they were superb for island hopping, albeit painfully slow. You had visions of a steady headwind holding you motionless a thousand feet up in the air. The great thing about them was their visibility, you could see everywhere as it was an overhead fixed wing and had large portholes. Coupled with the fact that they rarely flew above four thousand feet, given the shortage of distances involved. It was a real joy viewing what was and went on below, be it on land, beach or sea.

Max left to check his aircraft. After about twenty minutes and being replete on pastries and coffee our flight was called " Our International flight to Salt Cay is now ready for boarding". Mark you the 'International'. It was in truth not much more than a five minute domestic flight, but it sounded impressive. Why not? We boarded the ten seater and took off surprisingly quickly. There wasn't much scenery en route to take in because we were there almost before you could blink.

Then the fun began. There was a donkey avidly munching some growing weed half way down the runway. I say runway but it was more like dust and gravel. We circled once, twice, three, four, five times (about fifteen minutes in all) and were beginning to think a trip back to Grand Turk was the inevitable. But on the plus side we had an aerial view of Salt Cay. It was like a small model village with neat white houses dotted in places and paths come roads winding clearly around. The beaches were pure white. It just had an appealing unspoilt neatness to it, decidedly uncluttered. I knew I was going to like this place.

The donkey at last moved on and we landed and what passed for a terminal was in fact a hut with another donkey idly standing by it, totally uncurious as to what was going on. I suppose he passed for what passport/customs control there was, as no one else had bothered to turn up. We must have waited about ten minutes when a truck idled along. The aircraft having taken off as no one was getting on. It was our transport to the Windmills Plantation, to be our home for the next two days.

Chapter 16

Salt Cay

After about a three minute trip we were at the entrance of 'Windmills'; named after the windmills that serviced the salt raking industry, long since defunct. You entered first of all through what seemed a fenced barricade and then after about fifty yards saw about three grouped buildings, neatly set apart, with a main thatched restaurant cooking and seating area.

That mundane description simply doesn't do it justice. It's not even correct to call it a hotel. The buildings were the prized project of the owner, Eddie Shoestring, an award winning American architect. He had considerable experience of building hotels in the Caribbean with special themes and in this small development of some six to seven suites, he had modeled them on different styles found throughout the Caribbean Islands. The interiors reflected this and if they had a common connection it was rustic luxury.

Being Salt Cay no one locked anything and you simply helped yourself to drinks behind the bar and lay back in hammocks or sofas to take in the relaxation of it all. Having paid one price at the outset upon booking (seemingly high, but actually great for value) the subject of money was not thought of again. The food was cordon bleu at the highest level. Quietness was a respected attribute of the place; can you believe it, no phones or computers. You could idle away your time, read or chat as the mood took you.

Nowadays you go to resorts and find entire families sitting at tables, ignoring each other, hands clutching iPhones, eyes glued to the screens. As if they were on a permanent trip of Nytol. Conversation was still alive then, but only if you wanted. Modern day youngsters would go squirrels at this; shuddering at the thought of being without their electronic devices or perhaps even at the thought of having to make conversation. Far easier to text your friend sitting next to you! The parents usually being not much better.

Windmills fronted a beautiful beach with volumes of sand. A little unusual as it steeped quite a bit into the sea, where the sea surf was pretty active and swimming just offshore a little found you in quite deep water. Not unpleasant, just different.

In the evening the place was cast in a delightful soft amber light hue. The actual dinner served up was to die for. The sort of meal you actually remember and where it is an actual aesthetic experience as the delicate morsels pass across your palette to the accompaniment of fine wines (no supermarket plonk here thank you, Chateau Vinegar was taboo).

Eddie was, like most people who enjoy hosting, a good raconteur and had boundless amusing stories to tell. Strangely enough it wasn't that which stuck foremost in my recollection. He had a game he liked to engage his guests in, by getting them to successfully work out what a particular nautical item was. It was hanging in a corner outside the bar. It was round with odd protrusions on it and a hole at the side. Apparently only three guests down the years had worked it out correctly. Number four to guess it turned out to be my wife. She has that curious logical Sherlock Holmes type faculty of analyzing things, which yours truly clearly didn't have, at least certainly not on that occasion.

In fact the paradox to the episode was that I had had too much delectable wine predicated by more rum punches that I cared to admit to throughout the day and well, was out of it, to use the polite expression. Quiet , but just beaming stupidly in a pixilated fashion.   Anyway, the consolation being I slept well that night. We were all sworn to secrecy as to the objects identity once disclosed. In my case the next morning as told to me by my wife.

There has to be something about Salt Cay, because when I woke up I didn't have a hangover and was eagerly ready to get on with our exploration of the Island following a Scottish style breakfast; porridge, bacon, black pudding, fried eggs, sausages, mushrooms, tomatoes, toast, real marmalade (the Seville type with chunks), and tea. The only thing I didn't have were hash browns. They wouldn't fit on my plate! As to getting around, the choice was either Shanks pony (walking) or bicycles. Needing to walk off the breakfast the former was the decision.

Walking down the dusty road from Windmills and seeing the little white houses with their cross framed windows, small doors, low walled boundaries and shingled roofs, you really felt everything was somehow in a miniature perspective and it was like walking through one of those model villages you sometimes get in the U.K.

There was almost no one in sight and all was quiet save for the occasional braying of a donkey or dog barking. Once in a while someone would be tending to something outside their front door or you would pass someone walking to somewhere and it was invariably a kindly good morning exchanged. The sun beat down relentlessly with brilliant reflection from the ground.

There was little in the way of modern innovation; Salt Cay only got full time electricity in 1982. We came to the District Commissioner's Office. For Salt Cay a quite impressive white stone building, with the Commissioners bicycle parked outside against the stone pillar at the gated entrance.

Somewhat further on we stumbled upon the Mount Pleasant Guest House, run by a kindly and hospitable local by the name of Edgar Chanting. His family had owned it for generations and it was very popular with a select number of divers and the odd visitor who knew of its existence. It seemed that wherever you looked on Salt Cay everything was within sight which added to its attraction.

One of the oldest Buildings from the salt raking days was the White House. An imperious mansion like structure made of white stone. It was probably about a hundred and fifty years old (actually I am beginning to realize that everything is about one hundred and fifty years old in this book) and its ownership had remained in the same family since its construction. The current owners were two elderly ladies, the Sarrier sisters, who then lived in Massachusetts and occasionally visited their ancestral home.

It was fascinating and the Commissioner, Princey Lofton, a very courteous official, kindly gave us a tour. It was in essence preserved as a museum; everything was credibly left as it had been in the nineteenth century and in pristine condition. The downstairs consisted of a massive chamber supporting the entire upstairs and filled with salt; as had been the case in the salt raking days. The salt there could well have been a hundred years old. So valuable was it as a preservative for foods that it was, as already mentioned, called 'White Gold' and fortunes were made by the owners of these enterprises. (The word salt comes from the latin word salarium and Roman soldiers were paid with salt; hence the word salary). This was definitely the place time had forgotten.

A film was made on Salt Cay back in 1941, I think it was called Bahamas Passage and was something along the lines of a romantic thriller; involving stars at that time, one being a popular actor called Sterling Hayden. A financial windfall also came to the Island back in the late nineteenth century around 1896, when an American barque (ship) called the Pilgrim ran aground on the treacherous reef to the south and had a large consignment of coal which gave salvage profits to the Islanders.

The most famous wreck however lies some fifteen miles to the south of Salt Cay; it is where the Royal Navy ship HMS Endymion lies having been wrecked in a storm back in 1790. It's artefacts (chains, anchors etc.) identifiable and are a divers delight. In fact the person accredited with its discovery was, I believe, our very own Curtis Lemar, our learned and established historian from America. The discovery may only have happened in 1982, if my memory serves correctly. The warship had served in His Majesty's Navy for some eleven years, being successively engaged in many battles all around the globe, only to end up there one stormy night.

You cannot mention Salt Cay without referencing one of its most famous claims to fame. Whale watching. Every year, especially in February, hump back whales migrate and their passage takes them very close to the Island. Chartering boats and getting close to these magnificent creatures is a must experience I am reliably informed, as they get very close. It is immensely popular with visitors and it is yours truly's one ambition to witness this. After all these years I should stop prevaricating and simply do it.

Getting back to the Windmills we were somewhat tired with the heat; it surprises you and you have to be leery of the sun and its effects. Hats and sunscreen being a must to avoid sunburn and heat stroke. Water being the third rule. The afternoon I spent idling on a lounger verging on the beach when I noticed I had a neighbour about twenty feet away in a hammock slung between trees reading a book. He got up to stretch and introduced himself.

Herbie Wallbanger was a lawyer with a practice in Washington DC and this was his favourite haunt to come down for a few days to unwind from the stresses of working there. He was a tall exceedingly thin man with keen alert eyes. This was his Shangri-La where he could recoup. Actually he turned out to be a friend of Eddie's and an investor in Windmills. Although friendly he didn't say much but asked polite questions out of curiosity. I sensed he was a man of ability and its interesting how when you do meet people in life who are genuinely talented, they do not feel a need to advertise themselves or what they do let alone what they have achieved. Small world though as it happened, he knew two of my colleagues at my old practice in London and was complimentary about them, which did not surprise me. As it turned out the night before he had drunk more than I did with a resultant hangover.

We had another wonderful evening at dinner and next morning I hit the jackpot so to speak at breakfast with a selection of smoked kippers (an English delicacy). Sadly it was time to leave about midday and we caught the flight back to Grand Turk.

This time our captain was one of my favourites, a local by the name of Randy Whiskabout. He had three brothers and they were all excellent pilots and came from North Caicos. Although a short journey back, I was sitting next to Randy with alternate controls and joystick in front of me. Knowing my interest in aeroplanes and flying he offered me to takeover for a momentary spell which was great. But we had a lady passenger at the back who became decidedly agitated at the prospect of her fate being entrusted to my hands so I relinquished control immediately to allay her nerves. What a sensible woman.

We must have got home within thirty minutes of our take off from Salt Cay. So much for our sojourn in the quiet lands and now back to the bright lights and hustle and bustle of Grand Turk, joking, but by comparison it was.

I feel a short epilogue about Salt Cay is justified. It continued as a delightful get away for years thereafter. But in about 2007 the Islands were generally hit with a wave of investment projects, some of which proved dubious and unfulfilled. In the case of Salt Cay an East European tycoon wanted to buy virtually the whole place and turn it into a modern resort. Although it failed, Windmills unfortunately became a casualty and was subsequently demolished.

It's a theme all too prevalent nowadays, where things of true value are sacrificed on the altar of greed and monetary ambition. It was truly a great loss, but at least we have our fond memories. From time to time people have gone over to live there, but as enchanting as it is there is a great difference between visiting or vacationing somewhere as opposed to living for a lengthy period of time and save for a few exceptions the stay usually comes to an end. Nevertheless Salt Cay has something truly special and irreplaceable.

Chapter 17

Goldmining, Wind And Banking

In the morning there was a rat a tat tat at my office door. It was unusual to get anyone let alone this time of the morning, it was about eight o'clock. Through the frosted glass in the front door I could vaguely make out a diminutive figure and pixy like head with seemingly pointed ears. Opening the door I realized it was Woody Nutpequer, the last person I would be expecting.

I had in fact encountered him in Barclays Bank in Nassau when I was there. He was one of those irrepressible personalities and we were standing in a line up for service. He readily engaged me in conversation although I wasn't looking for it but politely responded. Somehow I seemed to get his entire life story in the twenty minutes or so we were standing there. He was probably one of those egotistical types who thought you intelligent and pleasant even though you weren't saying much. I was in fact a sounding board to himself. But he was pleasant and upon finding out I was going to Turks and Caicos asked for my details, little thinking anything more would come of it.

Few people carry their curriculum vitae in their back pocket and he produced a newspaper cutting from 1955 reporting one of the biggest gold mining discoveries in Canada's history in the northern part of Ontario. He was the named discoverer and the owner of the company having title to and running it. This fellow was the real McCoy so to speak.

He was slim and apart from his extended and rather pointed ears, had a broad forehead, straight hair plastered to the side and with what looked like Brylcream (an oily hair tonic popular in the fifties). His complexion was almost bleached white and he looked somewhat anemic. His voice was quite high pitched and had a sort of staccato, machine gun like, rapidity to it. Here was a bundle of nervous energy and his eyes seemed to roll as he spoke. He wore a short sleeved tropical shirt outside white trousers with the accompaniment of white shoes.

Woody's walk caught my eye as he strolled a little bit like a sailor having hit land after a long voyage, sort of rolling from one leg to the other. He oscillated between legs kicking them out and shaking his foot with each movement. Almost as if someone had dropped an ice cream down the inside of his trousers and he was trying to rid himself of the cold substance.

We were in my office by now and there was purpose to his visit. He had been researching wind farms and thought the Islands might be a suitable location given their windiness. You can see today how this industry has mushroomed into a gigantic multi- million dollar affair. He was ahead of the game so to speak.

However what he said next tended to cause my blood to freeze. He had met a returning resident on the plane here and he considered him to be a genius. It rather reminded me of Peter Sellers who was always remonstrating with his pal Spike Milligan who thought every Tom, Dick and Harry he met was a genius.

I was able to help him with some international business he needed (and through his in house counsel in Toronto that endured for some years successfully). But on this windmill project all my red flags went up and I declined involvement politely indicating that this sort of local work was not exactly my forte, which was true.

Woody mentioned that his bank in Nassau had provided a letter of introduction to their branch here and that I would also hear from the local manager to verify all of this. A bit presumptuous I thought as I scarcely knew him till now, but now I had some details so what the heck. He beetled off saying he would keep me in the loop as it were as to what was happening and we agreed to have dinner that evening. Meanwhile I had to go to the bank myself.

I strolled down to Front Street and the bank was located just after Cable and Wireless, the communications company, and not far short of the Post Office. It was a fairly small white building, very old, and I had seen its like when I was on holiday in Kenya some five years earlier. In fact that Kenyan branch of Barclays was in a small provincial town actually on the equator. It was white , dusty and drenched in sunlight.

I walked inside and there came a welcoming bellow from Mick Sturdypurse the Manager. A big bear of a man who rather minded me of that wonderful astro physicist Neil De Grasse Tyson (who made science so interesting on television). He was from St. Lucia. His door was always open reflective of the pleasant personality he was.

Try that with any bank manager today. They are usually insulated behind layers of bureaucracy (a firewall so to speak) and if you are lucky to see them they are usually dry and matter of fact following bank guidelines etc. Mick was the old fashioned type, interested in how you were, could you afford what you were doing and generally giving sound advice. Today banks just want their customers money and always looking for ways to appropriate it. Advising small customers to borrow when in fact they shouldn't and when things go wrong the banks jump in to asset strip what's left, often resulting in homelessness and ruination for families. They have also been extensively fined for selling fraudulent investments schemes to their own customers!

Of course at the other end of the spectrum they positively salivate over big customers. How many times do you read of their illicit activities at the higher levels, banking for dubious rich characters, fixing the LIBOR rate (fraudulently altering the rates at which the banks lend to each other). And when they are fined, although the sums seem astronomical to the likes of us, it is a mere parking ticket to them and a heads up to get up to the same racket again. The fines by the way are paid out of your monies. Don't believe all that advertising garbage they spend millions upon. They are moribund of any conscience. Don't you just tire of reading about these miscreant chief executives, collecting honours, gold plated pensions and lucrative share option schemes, when their conduct has virtually ruined the institutions they were custodians of with complete impunity for their actions. One Bank had to be wrongly bailed out in 2008 by the State of Qatar!

It's interesting how elected governments squawk at this behavior but do nothing about it. Lobbying is the name of the game nowadays, where large corporations bribe politicians and powerful functionaries to get the laws and deals they want. You could see the Barclay Brothers, the founders of Barclays Bank back in the eighteenth century, who were Quakers, turning in their graves at the antics of today's modern banking pariahs. They wanted to make money yes, but also viewed their roles as a catalyst and lubricant to society's business. Sorry, but that's all a sore point with me. How life has changed!

Actually in those days you could open a deposit account and get a twelve per cent interest return. Nowadays, thanks to the cartel racket the banks run, you are lucky if you get point five per cent. That was my real reason for being there. Mick then brought up the subject of Woody and the letter he had received from head office. He was to render any services that might be required. "Have you seen what this guy is worth" said Mick; almost rubbing his hands with invisible soap. No I said, but I hope he's careful and Mick nodded in agreement.

Leaving the bank I almost immediately bumped into Cyril Fixit a local builder who had been awarded the contract to build the new bank, which was to be constructed almost behind the existing one facing Pond Street, rather than Front Street and the sea. Everyone was glad he had this work as he was universally popular. He had some teething troubles in his early years in construction though. He had built about four bungalows up on the Ridge a few years previously, in a sort of compound. It was for a very nice Bermudian family.

We went to dinner there once and you couldn't help noticing that the door frames, instead of being perpendicular, were in fact angled at about eighty-five degrees. Molly who owned the place regarded it as a special talking point feature. Clearly it was the spirit levelers fault. But that was nothing compared to the shock they got when they moved in. When turning on the rear element to the cooker the television came on for some reason. Haywire electrics you might say, but it was sorted out. Cyril had come a long way since then and when the new bank was completed he had done a splendid job.

When I got back to the office Woody was waiting to introduce us to his new partner, Wally Watchit. Wally was one of those characters you could easily envisage idling his time in a chair on a side walk in some small mid-western town, looking to see what might float by. He was a short tubby little character, with a John Deere hat and corresponding short sleeve shirt with matching insignia. He had an extended stomach as he leaned back in his chair in the office. He had a generally swathy appearance and was sucking something that looked like a straw.

In fact I am not sure whether he said anything as Woody did all the talking, constantly calling his new found partner a genius as he rattled off his attributes. Bottom line seemed to be that Wally had previously worked at the now defunct Pan Am Base and was generally regarded as a Mr. Fix It All, which was very handy for the Island. Out of politeness I feigned interest, although I must have had a somewhat disconcerted look about me; something along the lines of an Englishman realizing with dread that he has no alternative other than to speak French in a particular situation. Having recused myself Woody mentioned that Wally had an existing legal contact so there was no problem. At last they got up to go and I ushered them out of the office wandering off into their sunset of future exploits together.

Dinner was at the Kittina Hotel where Woody was staying. In fact throughout the years I knew Woody I gained the firm impression that he stayed in hotels all the time; almost like a Howard Hughes so to speak, but without the reclusiveness (actually the latter trait might have served to keep him out of some of the scrapes he got into).

He was interesting to listen to. He had been in on the ground in the jungles of Panama and discovered one of the biggest motherloads of copper ever found. He actually gave my wife an emerald ring at dinner; goodness knows how he happened to have that to hand. Generosity being one of his traits as well.

He also knew about money and stocks and for the first time

I actually learned what it meant to short trade in stocks. It has to be kept in mind that although being a lawyer in the City of London my speciality was property, trusts and corporate work and never ventured into the financial aspects of dealing with money. Actually come to think of it I often regarded myself as a sort of barometric guide as what not to do; do the opposite to me and you will be alright. Okay, a bit far fetched, but you get the general point.

It's also worth mentioning that there was, not long previous to those days, a contrast between the North American enlightened approach to investing as opposed to the situation in the U.K. Up until Thatcher came to power in the UK in 1979, most Brits were insulated in their understanding of such matters. For one thing the UK economy was smaller and it owed the U.S. heavily in terms of borrowing from them as a result of the Second World War. In fact at that time it was outstanding and still was up until just a few years ago.

In addition we had exchange control (you could hardly take any money out of the country), so international perspectives for investing scarcely existed. Consequently, for the average Brit, their notions of investing were for the most part confined to post office savings accounts, purchasing premium bonds for the national lottery (known as Ernie) and the weekly dabble on the football pools. Conversely their North American counterparts from an early age were schooled in the wisdom in investing in the stock markets to protect their future.

When Margaret Thatcher came to power she abolished exchange control within twenty-four hours and opened the flood gates for a new type of capitalism, until then virtually unknown in the U.K. Well, in any event that was certainly my take on the situation. It was some time before we would see Woody again.

The corollary to the Woody/Wally windmill story made for grim listening. It was a few years later, when we were then living in Providenciales, and we met Woody on a visit to Toronto. Apparently as well as being a partner and really the only one on the spot, Wally had sole signatory capacity on the bank account opened for the venture. Woody had fed about three million dollars into it over about a two year period. A plane had been bought, there were no windmills, no assets and of course no Wally.

Woody did arrange to give us a tour of the Company's offices; located in a modern tower complex downtown and in the heart of the financial district in Toronto. The offices were palatial and high up. Everyone there was very courteous and obviously Woody was treated reverentially. He was not an operative as such but had his large shareholdings and received handsome dividends.

We were shown in to meet the CEO, a young pleasant chap who happened to be an accountant and a lawyer. When Woody was distracted, which was most of the time, the CEO looked in my direction smiled and winked. Memories of Nelson in Trafalgar Square came flooding back to me!

Chapter 18

Prime Rib Night

It was Friday and Poets Day (affectionately known in London as an acronym for push off early tomorrow's Saturday) something which as a partner in a business you had a tempered view of as it wasn't an automatic entitlement. For us it was PRN Night (Prime Rib Night) when Al Allyoucan really excelled himself. But first the daily chores lay ahead. We had to collect our new computer at the shipping office. In addition I wanted to visit the Land Registry, as although we did not do any property work at that time it was useful to collect the relevant forms to always have to hand.

I was just strolling into Front Street, when I came across Bob Scratchit, one of the U.K. personnel who came out as part of the interim administration. You often met ministers and officials on Front Street and everything in those days was on first name terms. Not infrequently you would end up having a drink with say a minister in the Salt Raker Inn, chewing the cud as it were. Nowadays that still happens but less so as there are so many more people here and things just are a little more impersonal. Much like everywhere else in the world now.

Bob had one of those rich West Country accents which is

where he came from. He could have been something straight out
of the Archers (a very popular farming soap radio programme
in the U.K. on every Sunday when millions would listen in).
You could easily see the conversation drifting into topics such
as brucellosis and how the pigs were or how cattle market had
gone that morning. Actually the conversation was just pleasant
banter, but with his strongly accentuated accent I could even
have been listening to Robert Newton in his famous role of
Long John Silver (minus the parrot on his shoulder of course).

I reached the Land Registry, located halfway down Front
Street within the Government compound where the Chief
Ministers Office was (currently vacant at that time). It was a
low lying building (almost as if an elephant had once sat on it
and finding it uncomfortable had moved on). The sign hung
awkwardly over the door.

I went in and it was dark; I half expected a bat to come
screeching out at me. Millicent Postlewit was the Registrar, a
large jovial lady always seemingly at ease with life. Her trusted
assistant was her Deputy ElVira DeVille. By contrast a thin
lady, slight with big spectacles and possessed of a somewhat
prominent set of teeth. She was clearly someone who knew her
stuff and suffered no fools gladly. Not someone to get on the
wrong side of either.

Although I was first into the Registry, a big Texan man
waded in before me up to the counter and shouted "Service"
to which there was no response. He thumped the counter
and made known his demand again only louder. Throughout
this demonstration ElVira was seated sideways onto him at
her desk clearly preoccupied, and certainly wasn't going to
be distracted by this bellicose oaf. He demanded to see his
title deeds, as if that made the difference. Eventually ElVira
turned to him and said emphatically "This is my Registry and

I am closing it as I have to go shopping", end of matter. The Texan was nonplussed and ushered out like a confused sheep. Meanwhile I had grabbed the forms I needed and likewise extricated myself.

On a later occasion a somewhat high powered land valuation officer, Eric Vin Floppen, had come out to do what was supposed to be important work for the Government from the U.K. He must have trodden indelicately on ElVira's sensitivities because she barred him from entry to the Registry. The poor fellow was distraught and virtually reduced to tears, being frustrated in carrying out his assigned duties. The lachrymose official had no alternative and lamely went back home. I fully understood the regime at the Land Registry.

Walking back to the office I met another official. Stan Scrivener. He wasn't new but was in effect the accountant and comptroller for Government. Stan was a small wiry man. He had actually been in the Colonial Service as it then was (predecessor to the FCO) since 1939! His first posting had been to the Sudan at that time, which was a British colony then. What stories he must have had.

His nickname was Joe Vinegar, simply because he was exact in his methods and would not accept any laxation of standards. In short he was a hard character to put one over on. The approach of getting it to the nearest dollar would not suffice with him, nor any unexplained expenses, of which there must have been a few of. Otherwise a perfectly chummy bloke.

My computer I collected from Ronnie Flounder at his shipping office. All was paid and cleared and I took the boxes back in the Green Goddess. Setting it up was not as bad as assembling my desk I am happy to say. But having done so and followed every instruction meticulously, I just could not get it to function. Thankfully this time there wasn't some precocious smiling brat on the box boasting how easy it was to get going.

We must have been scratching our heads for at least half an hour over this, thinking who we could phone to get advice. Suddenly and on an inspiration my wife jiggled the plug in the socket and hey presto it was working. I loved the ruggedness and simplicity of those machines, MS Dos and all that. Now we could get ready for Prime Rib Night.

When venturing into the Turks Head Inn it was wise to adhere to the well known maxim of mind how you go. Quite literally, as there was always a distinct possibility of going through the floorboards. It had certainly happened to a few unsuspecting guests in the rooms above. The wood being old and rotten, Al had never somehow got round to replacing the floors. The main dining room was long, with a series of tables placed end to end resembling something along the lines of a refectory table in a monastery. But there was nothing monastic about the evening. There were also a series of benches put end to end for seating and you more or less took pot luck as to where you ended up or who sat either side or opposite you.

Al's fare was simple. First course delicious prime rib with baked potato in its jacket with either lashings of butter or sour cream. Afters, again simplicity itself; baked apple pie with ice cream. All cooked to perfection. An utter elixir as far as we were concerned, washed down with copious amounts of wine or beer.

Opposite now were sat Ron Feltcollar and Andy Cuffs. Both British police seconded to the Islands force but acting independently in their assignments; namely tracking illicit drug movements through the Islands. The main concern being trans shipment from Columbia and island hopping into the U.S. Not a job for the fainthearted you would think and certainly they were discreet about their activities, although as it turned out there were some limited and at times interesting permissible exceptions to this; especially after a few beers.

Both were powerfully built men, in fact it was difficult to detect a neck in either case. They were in their thirties, strong jawed and could almost have passed for brothers. They were refreshingly plain talking types, experienced and very street wise so to speak. Ron was a detective chief inspector from Liverpool; a real scouse as the slang puts it. Andy came from Newcastle and was a sergeant. We tended to see Andy rather more because he had brought his wife and baby daughter out and they often liked to be on the beach, where we saw them. Ron didn't like sand or the sea for that matter.

They were hard nosed, no nonsense types. Both were obviously used to working in tough areas where they came from. They reminded me of the characters you got in a very popular programme we had in the U.K. on the T.V. called the Sweeney, back in the Seventies. As tough if not tougher than the villains they sought out and meting back to them what might be received with interest. Both had broken their noses at some time or other. They also had a sense of humour and probably needed it.

I had met them before at these Turks Head Inn prime rib nights and often it was then that you would hear their anecdotes. Andy being the more vociferous of the two, with a strong Geordie (Newcastle) accent. I sometimes wondered how they understood each other (let alone us understanding them) as Ron had a strong scouse (Liverpudlian) accent.

On one occasion a prisoner in the local jail had escaped and with help had managed to get off the Island. Andy trailed him and eventually tracked him down in the northern State of Indiana in America. It was some two thousand miles away and he brought him back. Talk about the Mounties always getting their man! These guys were intrepid and I am also sure that they were armed and had to be.

They did have their trials and tribulations locally. On another occasion Ron and Andy were trying to organize training sessions for sea rescue for officers in the force. They were sending two for a course in Florida which involved helicopter rescue. It necessarily involved being submersed in a water tank and effecting a rescue. It was left to an official to choose the recruits for this. They were sent to Florida. There it was discovered that neither of the recruits could swim! Andy said he felt like bopping the official when he confronted him, about not questioning them whether they could swim. The official just grinned back. It was a total waste of money and the recruits could have drowned.

Both went home on leave periodically. Andy said that when he went back and met his colleagues in the pub (bar) in England he would be drinking with guys in all sorts of guises. Such as hippies who mingled with the drug taking fraternity there. He said he didn't dare recite his experiences in the Islands for the simple reason that his mates would not believe him. What those other experiences must have been you can only conjecture.

I did witness him in a more serious mode though. One afternoon I was leaving the office and Andy was concerned because he hadn't seen Ron in a couple of days. He was understandably anxious as very often they had to split their work duties. Luckily Ron turned up and fears were allayed. But it brought to mind the sort of jobs which they had.

Looking back at Ron and Andy I cannot help but think how policing has seemingly changed from those days to the current era. These were the tough sort that really rolled their sleeves up and went after villains. You can't help but feel how this has all changed; especially with the cut backs in policing that besets the police force in the U.K. and it's a philosophy which overspills to the Islands as they are responsible for law and order here.

There is a dearth of funds from the UK, in fact none now, and the consequences are evident with increased crime. The emphasis in the U.K. today seems to be towards sociological policing and senior officers crunching out statistics from behind a computer. No more cops on the beat, instead the ardent pursuit of politically incorrect crimes, which obviously entail less personal risk. Or relentlessly pursuing people long since dead and spending small fortunes in the process. Softer targets one supposes. There is also widespread closure of police stations and very little presence on the streets.

In some cities in the UK now they no longer investigate burglaries carried out at odd numbered houses in streets and only carrying out cursory investigations at even numbered ones. The very senior officers are paid handsomely and collect honours and gold plated pensions whilst recruitment at the basic levels is low because of lousy pay deals. Somehow the world has turned upside down in its priorities. Bring back the Ron and Andys of this world, you felt safer then.

It was a great evening and upon hearing footsteps up above in the Turks Head Inn, followed by a creaking of wood and sprinkle of falling dust, it was time to call it a night less a torso fell down on to the table from above. So we all departed having made an enjoyable start to the weekend.

As an epilogue to the place, it was bought by a Hollywood director about twenty five years ago who closed it and did it up to its original rendering. He would sporadically visit with family and friends. It looked nice but had somehow lost its character.

Chapter 19

Itchy Feet And Treading Water

Someone once said to me that timing is everything in life. Maybe not everything, but I could see the point. It certainly seems to have had a hand in shaping destiny. And so it was with Grand Turk. I somehow wanted to move on, given we had been there almost three years, albeit that the business had expanded and grown healthily. Perhaps somewhat quite like the people who had gone to Salt Cay to live and yet left. I knew I would come back, but something else beckoned or just call it itchy feet. Providenciales, lying to the western extremity was becoming the bread basket of the Island's economy and there were sound reasons for it.

Believe it or not, small though they were, the Islands were contemplating independence from the U.K. back in 1980 and as the severance present the U.K. was going to encourage Club Med to set up in Providenciales on the best beach in the Islands, build a new airport and a road connecting the two. Club Med committed and the airport and road were completed.

How on earth independence would have worked in those days, given the economic logistics involved for so small a country (some seven thousand souls), beggars belief. Actually the Islanders saw the sense in this and promptly said to the U.K. Government "thank you but no thank you, we will remain attached to you after all". End of that.

Provo's own population in those days was only about eight hundred or so but there was a growth factor; particularly with mostly North Americans coming to live there or simply having holiday homes. Everything about it had a sort of pristine appeal as there had been very little in the way of any development and it was much bigger than Grand Turk. It's most famous beach was some seven miles long and there was little to compare it to any anywhere else in the world! The future seemed to be there and we wanted to have a reconnoiter so to speak. We were going to the airport to book our flight when Tom Wapping emerged from the Salt Raker Inn and wanted a chat with us. He wanted to buy the Green Goddess as he had just arrived in the Islands as part of the accounting section of the interim administration and was in need of transportation.

It is probably no exaggeration to say that Tom was one of the largest guys you could ever come across. He stood about six foot eight inches tall and must have weighed easily in excess of 400 lbs, not blubber mark you, just powerfully built. He had a jovial rounded face, again with long bushy sideburns (they had gone out of fashion even then) and gold rimmed spectacles. It was impossible not to feel cheery when he was around. He was one of those career FCO types who had travelled extensively and I suspect lived life to the optimum. Even his voice had a sort of "Ho,Ho,Ho" Father Christmas ring to it.

He had played rugby at university, in the frontline of course; in fact he could have constituted the entire front line. His memento to those days being two false front teeth which he could easily extract. Tom also had a huge mop of curly hair. His wife, Deidre, a petite pretty lady who always wore skimpy shorts accompanied him to The Salt Raker and sometimes he would actually carry her in on his shoulder; I imagine she had a good head for heights.

To say Tom liked a drink was an understatement, specifically Becks German beers, and he could quite easily demolish a whole crate of them during the day; taking into account extended lunches and of course the evening. Booze never seemed to affect him adversely and he just got merrier. He had a plethora of good jokes and tales. Stress was an anathema to him.

Actually he did get a spout of gout once (unintentional rhyming) and as he said, he cut back from a whole crate of beer a day to one half, and the problem went away. So it was a green light to up the consumption back to normal and there was no further resumption of the gout surprisingly.

With what we were contemplating, move wise, we didn't really need the Green Goddess anymore and since Tom was desperate for transport an amicable deal was struck there and then and Tom was to acquire the car about a week later. It was a perfect match, the car and Tom, both being enormous and I had visions that he could easily have driven the car with the sunroof open and Tom's head appearing out of the top of the roof. In any smaller car Tom would have looked ridiculous.

So to the airport to get our tickets, for what was called the "patch run" hopping to all the main Islands going west culminating in Provo; where we would spend a couple of days sounding the place out. Molly ran the ticket side of things for the national airline called Turks and Caicos National Airlines, which pretty much made sense.

Molly was a very pleasant girl in a her twenties and very trimly in appearance, always wearing high heels, stockings, pencil skirt and a blouse; with accompanying large earrings and heavily made up but in a nice way. In short very comely. Her most noticeable feature were her nails and they were perhaps the longest I had ever seen but elaborately decorated with varnish. That's very popular in the Islands, but how she managed to pick things up or perform the other usual functions I really could not understand at first. However she managed with considerable dexterity.

She in fact did a myriad of other duties, something which was lost on Woody when he tried to phone the airline. She obviously couldn't man the phone all the time and in his frustration he promptly dubbed the Airline "Turks and Caicos No Answer". We obviously didn't have cell phones then. But you simply don't adopt that attitude when dealing with people in the Islands. In any event he had rung at lunch time, when in all probability and understandably Molly would have either been in our nearby famed bakery, having her nails spruced up or purchasing her barbequed chicken in foil lunch. Anyway it was simply fun to go down to the airport. Our flight was first thing the next morning; 7am to be precise.

Being late in the day we went back home and decided to go for an evening swim. There is a fascinating house just on the north side of the Salt Raker Inn and it always made compelling viewing for me when either going downtown or crossing over to the beach. It was positively ancient, large, but here's the real oddity, it was comprised entirely of old grey shingle. Now roofs that's common enough, but for the walls as well that's really strange. You simply couldn't detect anything modern about it. It may have had a name, I just can't remember, but for most of the year it remained closed up with the shutters down.

It was owned by a retired American couple, who lived most of the year in Portugal and then would come over for about a month or two and open the place up. They were very pleasant and loved the place. They were called Marta and Wilbert and before retirement, some ten years previously, had run very successful businesses in the U.S. quite independent of one another. The garden was well tended but the building was just one mass of grey shingle, almost an anomaly which you could easily pass by without noticing, unless the peculiarity struck you. It was the sort of place you yearned to know what was inside.

Actually there was more to this house. About a year previously I had been wandering up towards Duke Street one evening and struck up a conversation with an elderly gentleman coming in the opposite direction and towards the grey shingled house. His name was Filbert Merriweather and he had actually lived in the house when he was young back in the early nineteen twenties and a bit before then even. His father had been involved in the salt industry at that time and that had been the family home. Although the family could be traced back to Bermuda, several generations had lived there.

Filbert was well into his late eighties, but fully upright with no suggestion of slouch to him and he had a spritely walk. The family had moved to Canada some sixty years previously due to the decline in the salt industry. The advent of refrigeration had obviously hit the industry but as far as the Islands were concerned the product could be produced more commercially, effectively and on a larger scale in Great Inagua, the Bahamian Island lying some one hundred miles to the west of us by the Morton company which as previously indicated still exists to this day.

He came down periodically and Marta and Wilbert welcomed him as a guest when they were there. He dressed smartly in a light grey suit, Panama hat and had a well worn lined face with a somewhat weather beaten look about him; rather reminiscent of the old fisherman in Hemingway's The Old Man and Sea.

But the real point of interest in this anecdote was the house itself. Originally it had been by the sea, but after serious storms many years earlier it had been decided to move it back to its current safer position. This actually entailed putting logs under the foundations and rolling it back! Conjuring up visions of ancient Egypt and great obelisks being moved by the same method with the prodigious efforts of scores of labourers. Incredible, but apparently it worked. As to the sanitation and plumbing aspects, well you daren't go there, but obviously all worked out fine. Oswald and Leopold Discardi would never have attempted this with their ramshackle abode.

So much for the flashback, it was time for a swim. Now you might think it a bit daft for someone who doesn't really care for the beach and is a trifle nervous about the sea living on an island. Well actually sand does make my feet itch and I don't like the feel of the stuff. As to the water, I like it but upon entering each time I usually start hearing that reverberative drumming music from the film Jaws. After the initial fear I like the water, especially simply just treading, but continually keeping an alert lookout for an unexpected fin on the surface.

It was on this occasion I met an expert, staying at the Salt Raker. He was from the U,K, and being winter there and the weather somewhat inclement, had jumped at the opportunity to come out to the Islands and do an economic evaluation. We tend to get a lot of this sort of thing.

It was for the U.K. Government, but his source of employment was in fact the O.E.C.D. (Organisation for Economic Cooperation and Development). He was courteous in a sort of civil servant stuffy sort of way, certainly not offering a name. He had been out for a week and couldn't really think of much to report back on by way of recommendation save perhaps that it might be a good idea to introduce some form of income tax to improve revenue.

As politely as I could, I suggested that he revise the idea and certainly not be let it be known locally, less they found what was left of his torso being strung up by the nearest lamp post. I don't think it made any impact, but it did teach me something about his employer, because today we are simply festooned with these pests and their bid to rule the world and we are often left stuck with their rotten ideas (invariably self serving) and imposed in the form of laws we have no control over. By the way, the same happens in the U.K. with the E.U. and elected politicians there don't even bother to read the stuff as mentioned already. Anyway the explanation merits expansion as it greatly affects the Islands. I will try to keep it succinct as it can get boring, but it is nevertheless important to understand what goes on.

The O.E.C.D. was formed loosely in 1948 after the Second World War. In those days it had laudable objectives of trying to get war torn countries back on their feet; Germany being the paramount objective for this then. In 1961 it became more formalised and constituted some twenty-five countries, in the form of a formal binding agreement, which today numbers some thirty-five. It is a very close confederate of the European Union. Most folks don't think about it, but they should.

The member countries agree that whatever the OECD determines to do shall be enshrined in law for all the member countries, including colonies. The OECD is made up of unelected bureaucrats who virtually have tenure for life and run the whole thing. The people you elect to represent you in your own country play virtually no part in this process. So that a bureaucrat or group of them say in Brussels or Strasbourg (actually I think the OECD is based in Paris, and a nice place to be at that) can make laws that effect your very life without you knowing who they are or having any say on the issue; i.e. democracy turned on its head.

It was one of the revelations exhumed over Brexit with the

E.U.; without most of the electorate even knowing that the U.K. had surrendered its sovereignty and legal system to the E.U. (the same issues apply).

Interesting isn't it how back in the forties post war, when a consortium of countries (including Greece) not only agreed to lend monies to Germany to rebuild but forwent the repayment and now within the E.U. Germany is demanding Greece make ruinous repayments to atone for its economic misfortunes. Has flavourings of Shylock wanting his pound of flesh, especially as the shoe is now on the other foot so to speak. Anyway, that's the way the world works today and as a final thought, before I get back to my water aquatics, Thomas Jefferson said, "Tyranny takes hold when men of good conscience elect to stay silent". Let's leave it at that.

My intrepid expert having gone off to write his report, who should come down to the water next but Hank Casanove, an American diver who ran a diving business along the road, followed by his customary flotilla of pretty lady divers in their bikinis. That was usually the way of it after they got back off the boat from one of his diving expeditions.

Hank was one of the most casual and offbeat characters you could meet, very easy going; enjoying his insouciant life style. He looked like another Tom Selleck and the ladies adored him. He was a Vietnam Veteran, in fact I think was a navy seal i.e. special operative. He was much more congenial company than the recently departed expert. Holding a half drunken bottle of beer and puffing on one of his favourite cigarettes, French Gitanes, probably sacrilege to today's diving and healthy living fraternity.

On telling him I was thinking of taking a look at Provo he growled "whad ya wanna go there for, neo colony of the U.S.A". Quite rich coming from an American, but that was

Hank.' Grand Turk was his Shangri La and who could blame him. So I left it at that, looking forward to the morrow.

w

Chapter 20

Westward Ho

It's easy going away for just two days at least packing wise, going from one island to another. But as with anything in the Islands (my old friend Leopold called the place "contrived chaos", perhaps not quite) things do happen. Getting to the airport we found that the patch flight had been delayed for technical reasons for a few hours but we could get a lift to our first port of call, being South Caicos, with Arnie Roughlander. Arnie had his own private airline company , well one plane actually, and he often helped out the main national carrier when occasion demanded. Arnie's plane was an old Beechcraft twin prop made in the nineteen fifties. It was a strictly no frills machine and often carried cargo between the Islands.

Arnie must have been in his seventies and had flown Flying Fortresses during the Second World War. He was a rough diamond sort but highly experienced, he always got you down and usually up; joking, but I will explain why. He believed in maximizing his payload of cargo, but always got the judgment correct. On board we buckled in our seats, I think Arnie did but couldn't be sure. But in every nook and cranny of the aircraft there were items of cargo. It was quite simply heavy.

We taxied for take off, the engines sounding like washing machines in their spin cycle, and slowly Arnie eased the plane down the runway a bit, ready for the full throttle. At that point he reached to a six pack of beers, just behind the throttle, opening the can with a hiss and took a swig and replaced it. He then applied full throttle and we gathered momentum. Slowly, or so it seemed, we lumbered down the runway gaining speed. But having reached what I assumed to be about three quarters of the length, I saw no sign of lift and the engines roared. Almost running out of runway the fuselage perceptibly lifted and we were airborne, with the sound of branches brushing the underside of the aircraft. We had made it. Arnie turned and smiled. "Not bad Eh". His moth eaten baseball cap wet with sweat.

It was about a twenty mile journey across and true to form Arnie landed with a thump.

Actually if there are crosswinds pilots are meant to firmly hanker down, but I got the impression Arnie liked to do that anyway. From the map South Caicos looks a bit like an upside down tadpole. The runway there is quite long and may even have the potential to cater for jets. It was built by the U.S. forces during the Second World War and was used as a hopping route to get supplies to North Africa during the campaign there. For years the economy of South Caicos had languished, it's Bermudian salt raking days long since gone, although the salinas and derelict mills were still evident. It has some superb beaches on the eastern side and today there are some hotels which cater for a devoted clientele. Its first hotel was called the Admiral's Arms.

We walked through the airport to a waiting area for the next patch flight, so it afforded an opportunity to gen up on the place for the couple of hours we had ahead of us. I was surprised to find out that the airport had harboured a bank until fairly recently, although the details seemed very obscure. Someone had cracked the line that it was custom free banking for aircraft rapidly arriving and departing. Make what you will of that one. Everything had a decidedly dowdy appearance to it.

The Island had enjoyed a period of prosperity in the seventies when the first elected Government had tried to stimulate the economy there; particularly the fishing industry and tourism. Curiously enough some local dignitaries in conjunction with a minister were behind this and seemed to succeed for a few years. The interesting aspect being that the minister promoting the place was in fact an Irishman, Jinty McScinty I think, who was the only non indigenous member of Government to be elected. I don't know what happened to him. It seemed he was a surveyor by profession and clearly had visions on the development side of things there.

Talking of surveying, a friend, Rob Clarkwallis who was a surveyor, happened to mention that when he lived in South Caicos for about six months, years previously, and doing work for Government, he came across surveying records of a piece of land dating back to 1813. It had been carried out by a sergeant in the Royal Engineers then and it proved to check out one hundred per cent in terms of accuracy, with reference to today's modern equipment. Some sergeant and some surveyor!

Speaking of royalty, the Queen actually visited South Caicos in 1966. She may have been en route to open the Commonwealth Games in Kingston, Jamaica that year. The Royal Yacht Britannia was moored just offshore. In fact I managed to get hold of an old newspaper commemorating the visit and still have it. A donkey race was held in the Queen's honour and she presented the prize to the winner. One teenager who participated in the race went on to become a well respected functionary in Government and years latter was awarded the MBE for his services to Government. I know him, went to his wedding twenty-eight years ago and he is retired now.

One thing that puzzled me at first was why there were quite a few abandoned DC3 two engine aircraft about the place. These were transport planes made by the aeroplane manufacturer Douglas, affectionately known as Dakotas or Cabbage Kites (because of their infinite variety of cargo) and they were sturdy and reliable. These were first built in the nineteen thirties and longevity was their virtue. Some were still flying from the thirties and they saw extensive service during the Second World War.

The general consensus being that they were carrying illegal substances from further south en route to the U.S. and had crashed for lack of fuel in and around South Caicos. On flying in I noticed one in the sea on the Caicos Banks (our shallow shelf to the south of the archipelago) and another at the far end of the airport with collapsed undercarriage and bent propellers. But the best example was the one that had crashed just short of the Commissioners Residence and Office on slightly higher ground.

The story there was that, lacking fuel, the plane was rapidly losing height and a decision was made to lighten the load by hurling out the cargo, being bales of marijuana. It didn't work and the plane's nose ended up just a few feet short of the Commissioners residence. The pilot and crew members who had survived without injury, always maintained that their cargo was beef, so next morning everyone was searching for bales of narcotic beef!

I am not sure what happened to the Admiral's Arms. It was said that at one later stage it functioned as a sort of university for young ladies studying biology in the U.S and who would visit to improve their studies. Rumour also has it that when that happened lads from the other Islands would find excuses to visit South Caicos to beef up on their own educational faculties. All sounds a bit disingenuous though. Our patch flight had arrived and so we moved on to Middle Caicos.

In getting to Middle Caicos we had to fly over East Caicos. I am not sure of this but it may in fact be the largest Island in our chain. Many years ago, in the nineteenth Century, there were efforts to generate the rope industry out of the abundant sisal plants that grow there. There are scarcely any remnants of occupation but there are descendents of the cattle which were brought over at that time. The sisal industry floundered and save for Monty's escapade at living au naturale there, little else had happened. It does have one of the finest large beaches you could find anywhere.

You almost immediately fly over Middle Caicos. It should be added that, with the exception of Grand Turk and Salt Cay (which are all separated from the Caicos Islands and Providenciales, by the deep tract of water being the Turks Island Passage), there are ambitious plans to link them all up with causeways and between North Caicos and Middle Caicos this has already happened with considerable effect.

Middle Caicos airport is a short runway and wherever you are destined for you need transport.

Quite close are some limestone caves that go very deep and I believe from memory there are ancient paintings and inscriptions. Lucayan or Taino Indians were also inhabitants going back many centuries, that is until Columbus and his successors exterminated them. You have to be careful going through them and use a torch as I virtually got concussed on one occasion when with a friend we bumped into each other headwise and unwittingly. Strange how when you hurt yourself it can be a source of unending amusement for third parties looking on. Mind you the antics did look a bit Laurel and Hardy like.

Just north on the coast from there lies Mudjin Harbour. Frankly it looks like a Cornish Cove, with high cliffs in a curve and majestic out rocks into the sea. The surf is dramatic and you have to be very weary of undertow currents. The effect is further dramatised by a long magnificent beach stretching off miles to the east. Offshore it also reminds you of the north coast of Cornwall in England. A vista miles away with far reaching rocks and crashing surf. The place still unspoilt but with the additive of neat little cottages for guests to stay (principally on a self service basis) high above the cliffs.

To go to either North or Middle Caicos nowadays takes you back the thirty years and more to the way things were. There is a delightful emptiness and tranquility to them. Further east from where we flew lies the small settlement of Conch Bar and then Bambarras and at the most eastern tip another one called Lorimers. These are delightful old communities really unchanged in many decades. Bambarras is renowned for its splendid seafood lunches.

Somewhere between Bambarras and going east over part of the north coast of East Caicos a ship went aground in the eighteen sixties during a storm. It was a Spanish transport ship and its cargo were slaves going to Cuba. Unfortunately Spain still adhered to that dreadful practise then. Since they were on U.K. soil they were emancipated and settled there. There were already other inhabitants because loyalists from the American War of Independence had also settled some eighty to ninety years earlier. There are still the old ruins of plantations on both North and Middle Caicos. They had tried to grow cotton but a type of weavel had played havoc with the crops so their economic resources dwindled.

On the subject of slavery, although emancipation was enacted in the early eighteen thirties in the U.K., one of its greatest proponents being the famous abolitionist William Wilberforce, due to parliamentary prevarication its real effect wasn't felt until some seven years later. Incredulously the Government in London saw fit to compensate the slave owners, in all its colonies, with something in the region of twenty million pounds (an astronomical sum by those standards then). You might have thought those funds could have fostered a better life if sensibly distributed to the emancipated slaves. True to form pecuniary considerations ever outweigh moral ones, as is evident today

There is a fascinating biography written by a Mary Prince written around the end of the eighteenth and early part of the nineteenth century. She was born into slavery in Bermuda, taken to Grand Turk where she suffered terrible deprivations and harsh treatment and then taken to Antigua and back to the Islands again. Anything written first hand beats third hand attempts and it makes for harrowing reading. She did however end up in England where she was emancipated and deservedly respected at last and endured some peace and comfort in her latter years. You marvel at the ability to forgive. Back to the airport if you can call it that and the five minute flight to North Caicos.

North Caicos is a small airport again, but on one occasion a Pan Am flight, making an inaugural flight to Providenciales didn't think so. The pilot was descending towards the runway when residents of the Islands on board realized his mistake and had to beseech hostesses to notify the guy up front that he was about to make history in the Islands and probably get very wet with the best of outcomes into the bargain if he landed. Put simply North Caicos cannot take an Airbus. Luckily he took notice at the frantic hoo hah going on behind him and veered away when it became very clear what he was attempting to do.

North Caicos consists of two well established old settlements; Bottle Creek in the East of the Island and Kew in the West. It is often called the garden of the Turks and Caicos Islands. It is certainly the most verdant Island and things that cannot be grown elsewhere seem to flourish there. The trees are taller as well.

It really offers a great days outing to hire a car at the southern end of North Caicos at Sandy Point and travel idly through North Caicos and across the causeway to the extremity in Middle Caicos at Lorimers. Even quickly it takes more than an hour but it is a delight to quietly journey along at a slow pace taking in the scenery and atmosphere. A weekend makes more sense, with guest houses in North Caicos and Mudjen Harbour in Middle Caicos. I really recommend it as it is positively therapeutic.

There have been fun and games in North Caicos as well, especially at election times. A few years ago we had a general election and the voting booths and halls were established. Voting continued throughout the day and in the evening the votes were to be counted. Then whammo, the lights went out and one of the boxes disappeared. It took well over an hour to restore power, by which time the voting box had mysteriously returned. Who knows what happened?

Another time it was the run up to an election and one of the candidates for the seat had introduced what was supposed to be a mega investor to the Islands. He was a huge man with a very loud, brash New York lawyer as his accompaniment and guide (the perfect second hand car or double glazing salesman type). They were going to build hotels on every Island "we're gonna do these things" the lawyer kept saying.

The resourceful politician had even got the investor to dress up as an arab sheik (hiding a crew cut underneath) and took him round North Caicos in a jeep for the general consumption of the electorate and distributing showers of dollar bills as he went. The only thing missing was a tin of motor oil under his arm. Funny thing was, the politician got in notwithstanding this antic, or was it because? We will simply never know.

Back in the early seventies a well known British construction company called Sprouts undertook the building of a hotel and in fact modeled it after a famous pub in Whitby in Yorkshire, England. It was called the "Prospect of Whitby" and was built on a breath taking beach on the North West side of North Caicos. It was a wonderful effort, totally in tune with the Islands character, and a great success for some years. In the early days, around 1972, Rob Clarkwallis had been engaged as surveyor for the project along with his colleague Wally Dundertops. Conditions were primitive to say the least and they had to share a caravan, with propane gas supplying the power and another caravan which did for the office.

This state of affairs had to endure for some months and when each got leave from the outbacks of North Caicos, they dived into the bright lights of Grand Turk. According to Rob, it was like a marooned mariner being rescued after years of isolation. Fortunately for him he encountered a policewoman newly seconded to Grand Turk, with similar views about the lack of entertainment in the Islands. Rob and she hit off and within twenty minutes they had rapidly adjourned to the Kattina Hotel where nature took its course.

Now there was a bar in North Caicos then, but it was about five miles down the road from where their caravan stood. The only transport they had was a giant road grader, which travelled at about three miles an hour maximum. Getting there during daylight presented no problem but getting back it was dark and the machine had no lighting. Having had a number of beers they guided the machine back standing or slumped high up at the controls. It had no steering wheel but two alternate levers for right and left. The engines gave a gentle hum as it went along quite silently.

Every so often someone would approach on foot with a flashlight giving limited vision. The tendency was to spot the giant grader only at the last second, whereupon there usually was a yell and the torchlight with the holder flew and peeled off into the bushes when they were aware of what they were up against. Next morning a local deputation asked them never to attempt such an escapade and crazy pub crawl again.

Rob later went on to live in Provo and became successful in property there. The Prospect of Whitby sadly closed for a number of years. It enjoyed a temporary new lease life in the late nineteen nineties, when a subsidiary of the mammoth Italian food company called Parmalite bought the hotel and did it up. It attracted scores of sun loving Italians. However when the Parmalite scandal broke and the company fell into liquidation the hotel closed and never reopened again. I saw it just a few years ago when visiting North Caicos and it was in a deserted and derelict condition. A very sad end for what had been a great project for North Caicos.

Chapter 21

Provo, The Huck Finn Isle

Taking off from North Caicos you head south and immediately encounter Parrot Cay. Actually it's a corruption of the word "Pirate" which was where Captains Ann Bonnie and Mary Reed hung out for the nearby freshwater lens to replenish their ships. A beautiful isle with pristine beaches to the west and inner mango swamps on the east side, approachable by the waterway there.

A few years back a well known character, Hank Puddinbasin had lived there with his Hungarian girlfriend, Countess Stomtofsky. Rather like Monty's efforts in East Caicos but they lived in a hand built shack there, got regular provisions laid off by boat from Provo, and without the need to do the au naturale thing. In fact they endured a lot longer. Today that isle is the internationally famous Parrot Cay resort, attracting celebrities either staying at the hotel there or having homes of their own built in seclusion on the incredible beaches.

Next in succession come Dellis Cay and Fort St. George, smaller islands. The latter with remnants of a fort but the cannons are clearly visible still in the clear azure waters. These date back at least two hundred years when the British had their tiffs with the French. There then follows the ultra secluded and exclusive Pine Cay which comes into view. Some of the wealthiest people (the sorts featuring in the top rankings of Forbes Magazine) have private homes there (you have to be vetted and accepted to get in).

This was the brainchild of a renowned architect Count Stomtofsky when he was alive (being of course the Countesses's husband and well before Hank did his thing on Parrot Cay, long after the count's sad demise). The theme is simplicity and all has a sort of rustic appeal. It's not even intended to cater for the luxury ambitions of the Parrot Cay Resort. Solitude in paradise has its price. Thereafter comes Water and Little Water Cays; homes to our indigenous large lizards, the Iguanas. A big tourist attraction nowadays, being only a stones throw away by boat from Provo.

Circling to the west before landing, you take in Provo. When you were young did you ever look at cloud formations or countries on a map of the world and find they took on the shapes of a particular animal or thing. For me Australia always took on the profile of a Scottie dog's head looking west. Well Provo to me seemed like an Alladin's lamp; handle in the west and the spout to the east (alright, a gravy boat to be honest). Whoever rubbed the lamp got his wish from the Genie called Mother Nature with what justifiably counts as the most beautiful and longest beach possibly anywhere in the world.

It's now called Grace Bay Beach and attracts tourists like flies to jam and eager to repeat the experience. The shallow azure waters add to this aided by glorious sunshine. Grace Bay lies along the north shore going to Leeward in the east. There is also a reef about a mile offshore which adds to the vista. There are other beaches such as Taylor Bay on the south. With further beaches on the handle and western part and Long Bay on the southern shore going eastwards again. In those days they were all virtually deserted.

In many ways Provo seems like an entirely different country to Grand Turk. The latter is essentially a tight knit community on a smaller island. Provo is about twenty two miles across, west to east and varying between two miles and half a mile wide, north to south. Provo has three original settlements. The Bight on Grace Bay, Five Cays to the south of the Islands. With Blue Hills running about two to three miles along the palm fringed coast of the western north coast of Provo. The latter very picturesque.

These were tightly defined communities in those days. The population of Provo could not have been much more than eight hundred Islanders with a sprinkling of expats. It befuddles the mind to contemplate how the people of these villages eked out a living down the years. One surmises at fishing and salvage work from the odd ship wreck. There was barely an airstrip for years and power and water supplies were very late developments. Many had to journey to Grand Turk, mostly by boat for essentials and health matters and the like.

What it must have been like to have been marooned there makes for chilling thought. On the southern side of the Island at more than one promontory there are carved in the rocks inscriptions by unfortunate mariners who found themselves in precisely that predicament. Their names appear with dates like 1714, 1758 and other dates both in the earlier and later centuries.

Apart from the going away present of the airport, road and Club Med from the U.K. Government, there had been sporadic pioneers down the years, lone entrepreneurs if you like, who had also contributed to the development of Provo. Back in 1966 a couple of pilots had flown over the Islands almost by chance. They had already developed a small hotel further north up the Bahamian chain of islands.

These characters were from the famous Dupont and Luddington families. They were taken with Provo and were able to conclude an agreement with Government to develop Provo along certain lines. I seem to recall an old photograph of their first arrival with actual equipment. It looked something like an old landing craft with a jeep and pieces of machinery and the like. From such humble beginnings did great things begin and that lead to Provo getting off the ground.

They built a friendly looking hotel called the "Third Turtle Inn" consisting of a bar, dining room and neat little cottages on the surrounding elevated ground at Turtle Cove. This was ideally suited on what became a little harbor and the route to it from the outer reef from the open sea necessitated dynamiting and blasting rock in the reef to make a cut, which became known as Sellars Cut.

The initial bunch of characters who spearheaded this project were called "the Seven Dwarfs" and to this day I still haven't figured out the reason for this; they were all pleasant enterprising guys and there was certainly nothing dwarflike about any of them. These and other pioneers really helped get Provo off the ground, although the extent to which it eventually took off would have astonished even their wildest expectations.

On this exploratory visit we needed somewhere to stay. In those days hotel accommodation was no problem as frankly there were so few visitors to the Islands. Club Med was up and running though. The options were the Third Turtle Inn, The Yacht Club, both in Turtle Cove, which was a specific point of interest to us as a base. There was the Mariners Inn on the south side near the docks. This had been built by a baker from Montreal. In fact all he wanted to construct originally was a bakery, but somehow he had been persuaded then by Government to expand his ambitions to a hotel, much to his chagrin at that time. We in fact opted for the Island Princess, the only hotel right on Grace Bay Beach, with splendorous views of the North Shore.

You would probably rate it between two and three stars, but that could be said for everywhere else and it had the basics which was really all we were looking for. The plumbing was noisy though, which explained a hammer by the washroom basin. When running water came there were the oddest thumping sounds in the pipes which somehow mysteriously abated once a few bangs had been delivered with the hammer. The shower was something akin to the surge of Niagara Falls and you hung on to a rusty rail for dear life, less you were swept away.

We hired a car from Toulouse Lebanger, a small wizened Frenchman who ran the only car rental business and chugged off on our exploration. It was an old chevy that rattled a lot and there was a sign on the dashboard "If someone needs a lift give them one as a matter of courtesy". Nice touch I thought, although today is a bit different and you do not see those signs on rental cars in the Islands anymore. Times have changed!

From an administrative point of view, Provo in those days was something of an outpost as far as Grand Turk was concerned. They looked upon it as a sort of troublesome child existing away from home. I won't exactly say it was an antipathy but there was always a sort of resentment and suspicion; rather along the lines of what was it up to and perhaps a bit of jealousy as well. An attitude that is even still there today. It was like a sort of Huck Finn doing his own thing against the establishment and was looked on as a place full of renegade cowboys beyond control. Neo colony of the U.S.A. as mentioned before, but in actual fact there were also a lot of Canadians, French, Brits and a splattering of other nationalities as well.

Government did have a District Commissioner, a very pleasant and able fellow, in fact the very same participant in the donkey race held in the Queen's honour in South Caicos back in 1966. I mention all this because as a matter of protocol our first visit was to see the District Commissioner, whose office was downtown. Downtown closely resembled an Australian outback cattle station and dust seemed to be everywhere. For some odd reason it also reminded me a bit of Kevin Costner in the film Dances With Wolves, when he finally discovers what the post he has to man looks like (way off the mark, but it was just an impression).

The most imposing and official office for our audience was the Managers Office of the local Barclays Bank. I thought, mistakenly as it turned out, that the District Commissioner would be hosting this in his. The Manager clearly having been turned out of his office. Instead the chair was occupied by a very serious, important looking and courteous gentleman by the name of Augustus Overlord. Of middle age and apparently the most important businessman in Provo and owner of virtually all of downtown. I also later discovered that he owned prize property on Grace Bay and the most important food retailing outlet. Clearly a man not to be trifled with. He asked very polite questions and seemingly satisfied with the answers, said it was a pleasure to make our acquaintance and wished us well with our endeavours in Provo. Marlon Brando in the Godfather couldn't have carried it off any better. So next stop was to view some accommodation and office space which we had in mind.

Turtle Cove was the place of interest, where the boating marina was with a number of small commercial outlets in the form of shops, catering for tourists, a small restaurant where you could also get your haircut, art shops, diving operations and in fact anything that might attract local or tourist money. The particular development was modern but in a pleasing sense. It formed a sort of quadrangle fronting the marina.

It had an upstairs facing the marina and there were two apartments available. One on the end with splendid views of the marina and looking east and the other adjoining with views of the marina. Both were superbly equipped with air conditioning, washer/dryer and every modern essential you could want. In comparison to Grand Turk this was sheer luxury. The building was new and open, with nothing claustrophobic about it. The rent was attractive as well. The idea being to have the one on the end as an office and the adjoining one for living in. It couldn't have been better and the development had a car park looking on to the marina.

Now for the landlord. Hyram Bigley the IVth was to say the least a man of substance; both financially and physically. I better interject here to give a slight preface for what follows. By now you will probably have formed the sound view that the person writing this missive is continually encountering blimps or Michelin men who are attracted to the Islands. Well it so just happens this is true, in a lot of instances, and I really cannot explain it. Maybe it's something about the place that attracts size and corpulence. To address the sex equality thing I had better also add that there are worldwide young ladies, trim and nimble in their early years, who grow up and upon reaching a certain age enlarge dramatically to emulate their mothers; rather like the cork being suddenly yanked on a self inflating life raft. Hence the expression for prospective husbands, 'always meet the mother'. Now I'm really in trouble.

Hyram was easily three hundred and fifty pounds and stood

about six foot. He looked a bit like a modern day Humpty Dumpty but somewhat mirthless as he never seemed to smile. Not to suggest that he was a bad egg (couldn't resist that one) but that was the way he was. There was also something of a bullfrog look about him as instead of a neck there was a bulging mass, rather like when a bullfrog puffs himself up. He was a superb businessman and had made a fortune in the insurance industry in the States. This was his retirement and he could only have been in his late fifties. He was also a very good landlord and looked after his properties, of which I believe he had several on the Island and beachfront at that.

His love was fishing and he had a magnificent custom built fishing boat moored in front on the marina with a smaller but still impressive one along side it. Apart from his financial acumen, fishing was his passion in life. He was also a no nonsense type and liked to get to the point. Shrewdness was a facet of his personality and I would imagine you would have to get up very early in the morning to get the better of him, assuming that was possible at all. He had a simple philosophy, give good cost effective service.

To his mind Americas greatest success story was the fast food industry which proliferates everywhere in America. He had a point and it might also go in part to explain the obesity problem which exists there. I mean you can scarcely drive a mile there without encountering a food outlet. Enough of that, we reached a mutually agreeable deal and we were to move in three months later around Christmas time.

As a measure of his being a successful man, his staff were good and there was clearly a loyalty factor there. He had a full time captain for his boats, Big Willy, a younger version of Hyram. They would communicate with each other from one end of the development to the other with forceful voices that would have put the Tannoy Systems out of business. Like mastodons bellowing to each other across a primeval swamp.

Everything concluded we spent the rest of the time just touring around and then got the late afternoon flight back home to Grand Turk. This was actually a move we were looking forward to and again it had an adventurous aspect to it.

Chapter 22

The Container Has Landed

The next morning walking down Duke Street I bumped into Ray Bridenorth, the retired engineer who lived there. In a sort of hallowed thrill voice he said "you know what's going to happen early tomorrow morning". Well of course I didn't but from his tone I momentarily wondered if it was something calamitous. "Halley's Comet" he exclaimed, "we will be able to see it about three in the morning and you won't want to miss it".

Such was his exuberance he reminded me a bit of that wonderful eccentric astronomer Patrick Moore, who blessed the U.K for years with his programme called "The Sky at Night." Actually you tended to watch it for his antics, let alone the astronomical content, which for me was pretty boring to be quite frank about it. Politely I said "fine that sounds really interesting, wouldn't miss it", disguising my disingenuous feelings and wondering why on earth would I want to roll out of the comfort of my bed at that hour.

At the appointed hour Ray knocked on my door and we went out. The quietness of everything was eerie. Then Ray pointed up to the sky and lo and behold there was a golden orb, a bit like an orange, slowly pacing its way across the heavens. It was somehow so neat rather than dramatic. In fact it was pretty as it had tiny golden stars spluttering from its cone and trailing gently back in its wake. The colour was spectacular, because, instead of the customary dark navy blue expanse, the whole surrounding area was a delightful royal blue which contrasted so well with the golden features of the comet and its sparklers.

I was truly grateful for this experience as it counts as a life long remembrance for me. I think Ray said it would not repeat itself for another seventy-five years. How that puts life in perspective. Imagine Napoleon or Charles 1 on its previous circuits or who would in the future. I thanked Ray, this time genuinely.

It's a funny thing that going directly west from Grand Turk to Provo you are only talking about a distance of some fifty miles. And yet some aspects of our move entailed far greater distances. Also the logistics of the exercise are surprising. It was mind boggling how much you accumulate over a period of just short of three years. Looking back in hind sight, what seemed simplicity itself in fact made the planning of an arab caravan an easier proposition. Much of the furniture and heavy items had to go in a shipping container. To Provo direct you might think. No way. It had to travel five hundred and seventy miles to Miami and then back again, schedules permitting, to Provo. A lot of smaller stuff would have to go in an aircraft, but I was giving Arnie Roughlander a miss this time. So I was on my way downtown to arrange all these matters.

I had reached Front Street and happened to gaze out to sea (I am always looking for distractions) and saw an unusual and yet what looked like a very purposeful vessel. It was certainly no luxury yacht. It must have been about one hundred and fifty foot long and although quite sleek, it had various pieces of equipment aboard. I think I could at least detect a small crane and winch. And then it dawned on me. I had read in the newspaper (yes, we have some very good ones at that) that our historian, Curtis Lemar, was putting together an expedition to try and find the lost wreck of one of Columbus's lost ships called the Pinta.

It seemed, as far as anyone could discern, that it had sunk some miles south of the Islands in what was called the Molasses Reef. This had great significance as the five hundredth anniversary of Columbus's landfall wasn't that far away in 1992.

Curtis himself was interesting. A very learned and erudite scholar (I think his alma mater was Columbia in New York) and yet so diverse were his talents that he had been a banker on Wall Street. He was also a delightful and fascinating character to meet with a marvelous sense of humour. To look at his deportment and demeanour brought to mind the Scott Fitzgerald character, the Great Gatsby. He undoubtedly had style.

Curtis, like so many of us, ended up staying in the Islands many more years than he had probably originally intended. He was a big hit with the ladies, but he also had a drinking buddy called South African Sid, who ran a car sales lot just off the Leeward Highway. Not to insinuate that they were inveterate boozers, but occasionally they would end up imbibing quite a lot, as happened one particular evening when they went out to a bar for a "good session". Now whilst Sid had a car of sorts, Curtis's preferred mode of transport was a motor bike.

On the way back home this time Sid chose to drive just behind Curtis on the bike just as a safety precaution. Approaching The Ramada Hotel, Curtis's arms suddenly went up in the air as if stretching, his hands completely off the handle bars, then he suddenly dived off to the left into some bushes. The bike went on a bit further and duly followed suit. Sid stopped and anxiously sought out Curtis who thankfully had not sustained any injury, but was completely out of it so to speak. Sid bundled him into the car and took him home, leaving the bike of course.

Next morning Sid called by Curtis's place to check he was alright , knocked on the door, Curtis emerged somewhat hungover and rubbing his eyes. A look of horror came over his face as he gazed across the yard ,"Call the police" he shouted, "Someone's stolen my bike"!

He had a truly great sense of humour which was put to good use, although the episode I am thinking of moves the time line on a bit. I think everyone remembers where they were when 911 occurred, much like the Kennedy Assassination. In the aftermath Bush and Blair invaded Afghanistan in a vain attempt to find Osama Bin Laden. It proved fruitless and instead they invaded Iraq upon a preposterous pretext. The latter event invoked much protest and resentment, because whatever Saddam Hussain's misdeeds may have been, he certainly wasn't behind 911 nor were any weapons of mass destruction found as alleged by Bush and Blair. We all remember the protests and they can a take a strange form as I discovered.

Now downtown in Provo we had at that time a little café called 'Mighty Morsels' where every morning folks gathered to partake in coffee and doughnuts. I happened to walk in one morning and there seated in front of me in the corner was none other than Osama Bin Laden himself. So you have it on the best of authority that he was actually here in Provo, munching doughnuts and slurping down coffee.

It was actually Curtis, dressed and made up. It was a brilliant take off (knowing him he probably spoke Arabic as well). A bit of a jibe at the abortive attempts of Bush and Blair to catch the original miscreant and perhaps more to the point an 'up yours' to them for the pointless invasion of Iraq, which cost so many lives needlessly. Something along the lines of the Scarlet Pimpernel comes to mind, "they seek him here, they seek him there........is he in heaven, is he in hell......that damned elusive Pimpernel." It was uncanny and shocked you when first encountering him, as he had done it so well.

Anyway enough of that, coming back to the Pinta expedition, for this enterprise Curtis had persuaded the world renowned salvage expert Ray Dredger to accompany him. He had quite a track record in salvage and in particular his discovery in 1981 of the sunken HMS Edinburgh. It was a cruiser in the Second World War carrying about a hundred million pounds worth of gold from Murmansk in the northern Soviet Union to the UK in payment for war provisions. It was sunk in the Barents Sea close on Arctic waters and this achievement in salvage was something of a revelation. So who better for finding the Pinta.

I met Ray once in a bar in Provo by chance. In fact I mistook him for an American. He was wearing one of those Nashville country and western cowboy shirts encrusted with sequins and had jeans to the accompaniment of pointed cowboy style boots. I had the shock of my life when he spoke and out came a broad Yorkshire accent. He was fascinating to listen to. Having worked his way up from humble beginnings and becoming one of the top commercial and much sought after divers in the world. One would imagine that he had become deservedly affluent as a result of his efforts. A considerable amount of time and effort were invested in trying to find the Pinta but unfortunately to no avail and it still lies somewhere out in those waters.

Curtis was a great proponent for the argument of Columbus's first landfall being Grand Turk, along with Alfie

Tryon, and serious arguments were defeated from a plethora of academics who claimed the Bahamas for that distinction. In boxing parlance Curtis and Alfie won on points in most peoples opinion (well to be quite honest, we are very biased here). David had overcome Goliath. Their scientific and Holmesian logic having proved most persuasive.

The time to the actual day of the move went in a flash and it was with no inconsiderable remorse that we said good bye to our office and home in Grand Turk. Even the container landed swiftly, taking just a few days up to Miami and back. The flight didn't end up in the water with all we were carrying on board and, all in all, it was a very smooth operation.

The only difficulty came in negotiating the staircase and entrance to the new office and home. The doors on both apartments were too narrow. For a moment you had visions of that Laurel and Hardy comedy when they are trying to deliver a piano up multi flights of steps where everything conceivable goes awry. Such small trifles were of no matter to Hyram, who got his trusty helper Lofty to go get a fork lift truck and commence delivering everything through the balcony and open sliding door at the front of the building. A master stroke.

The new accommodation and office were perfect. Now all that was awaited was the arrival of our new car. In Grand Turk you can just about survive without transport but in Provo, given the distances and how everything was strung out, that was not even on the cards. On this issue we had gone from one extreme to the other. From the largesse and grandeur of an old Cadillac to a brand new Citreon Deux Cheveux. Sounds crazy but it was in fact perfect, albeit very oddball. It arrived about two weeks later and its colour was a striking duo red and white.

Everything about it was unorthodox but was it practical. Negligible fuel consumption. It had a roll back top, flap opening windows. It sounded like a lawn mower when you started it up. It was spacious. The real accolade went to its comfort. The suspension was superb and you floated along the road. This was ideal because Provo in those days was for the most part dirt track, bumpy and ill serviced roads. We may have looked a bit of a laughing stock but certainly had the last laugh in terms of maintenance and durability.

What a lot of people do not realize is that the French Government laid down a particular set of peculiar requirements for Citroen when they commissioned its design. It had to be capable of safely accommodating a clutch of eggs for a farmer on its back seat, without them falling or cracking; hence its remarkable suspension. How about that for quality control! It was envisaged as a cheap car for farmers. Imported, the car had only cost four thousand seven hundred and fifty U.S. dollars and that included the customs duty of thirty per cent, and we have no income or capital taxes, so Government, needing its revenue from somewhere, placed a high rate of customs duty on imported goods and stamp duty on real estate purchases, and once only on acquisition.

At that point we were well and truly settled in. In retrospect the next three years were probably the happiest spent in the Islands. There was a pristine, uncluttered quality to life. Time seemingly didn't matter and there was no excessive bureaucracy and technical pressure that the current world thrives upon. Life was simply stress free and delightful. More especially the Islands were unspoilt. Those were the halcyon days there. It's incredible how mankind's interference with the natural order of things can irreparably alter that condition and not for the better. There's actually a word for it: "Progress"!

Having been installed for about two weeks, we thought we would celebrate the landing in Provo with a night out at Club

Med. It was a fantastic facility and in a sense a night out there was like getting off the Island altogether. An odd statement perhaps, but sometimes you do need a change of scenery and experience (it's called rock fever) and once the batteries are recharged you are ready to go on again so to speak.

The main feature there is the dining experience with copious amounts of excellent food and wine for a fixed entry fee of forty bucks a head. No limit on the amount of food or wine consumed. You sit at round tables each seating about ten persons which makes for congenial conversation whilst you sporadically slumber up for more food as your condition permits you. The same applies to the wine and the bottles are constantly replenished as they get consumed.

It's amusing because upon finding that you live on the Island you become an immediate source of curiosity to the visiting guests; almost like a rare species in a zoo. You find yourself dealing with lots of questions, most commonly "what's it like living in this wuuurrnderful place." It non plusses you a bit and you tend to get somewhat blasé in response, simply not knowing precisely what to answer back.

After the meal comes the show put on by the G.O.'s who run the place. It's good and often funny, even if a bit corny, but no one minds as everyone is having fun. The preliminary to the show usually has the chicken dance, a daft set of physical movements involving hands on shoulders and waddling like a chicken to the orchestrations of the G.O. leading the tomfoolery to this well known music. Everyone joins in.

Funny thing is I was taking off from Provo airport on the Pan Am flight to Miami once and the hostess was demonstrating the safety maneuvers. She actually was unwittingly parroting the G.O.'s antics on the chicken dance. A whole section of the passengers, fresh from Club Med going home, started following suit singing the chicken dance and mimicking the actions. The hostess simply broke down with laughter. One returning Medder saying "tell the pilot to hurry up the take off, the mosquitos are catching up" as we taxied down the runway.

Club Med don't accept money at the bar, so you had to buy beads in those days. Guests tended to go in the sea with the beads in their swim wear pockets, unaware that they often slipped out and into the sea. Now there is a current carrying things across the bay to the north eastern point beach of Provo and loads of the beads would wash up there. Guess what. Lots of residents would go up there, scour the beach and pocket the beads and have plenty of them for their drinks at the bar when they went for the evening. It must have seemed strange at the reception that none of the visitors were purchasing beads.

Talking of Pan Am, we had a visit from the CEO of that company some time later. He was incognito so to speak and was travelling with a client of mine who had bought property in Provo in my early days in Grand Turk. He had been a referral from a law firm I knew and although as a rule I did not do local property work it was hard to refuse. We got on very well with him and his wife and likewise with the CEO and his spouse, having had a thoroughly enjoyable meal at the Third Turtle Inn one evening.

He subsequently sold his land and at that time his business offices were in one of the Twin Towers in New York. 911 happened at least a decade afterwards and I tried to follow up with any contact details that were to hand, but to no avail. I just hope he wasn't a victim in that awful event. Probably he had retired much earlier as he had often spoken of doing. Now on to my first mistake, buying a boat!

Chapter 23

Boating With JoJo

I think earlier that I referenced J.K. Jerome's novel "Three Men in a Boat", basically a comedy which took place on the river Thames at the turn of the last century. It was a hilarious romp on the river by three pals who had never boated before. Well they had nothing on me. Although I simply adore boats to look at and even being on them, provided it is someone else's, but put simply, and I had to learn this through experience, I am something of a modern day "Jonah"; although perhaps minus the melancholic aspect thankfully.

It all started one Saturday afternoon when gazing down from my office window I saw a very neat eighteen foot or so fishing boat, looking down across over the other side of the car park in front of the development and discreetly moored at the jetty there on the marina. It had brown livery and a yellow stripe down the sides. A neat canopy, console and seat, with a fishing well for caught fish; not that I knew anything about fishing. It also had a fixed ladder at the side of the stern (I at least had some terminology to hand) and of course a sizeable outboard engine. It was the sort of thing that fired the imagination; especially given the Islands, their shallow waters and the opportunities for snorkeling etc. This whole concept positively wreaked of fun.

I asked Hyram about it and it turned out it was his and he was willing to sell it. In fact he did a successful sales pitch on yours gullibly and said I would have the time of my life (he wasn't joking, although probably not in the sense he meant). It was a great price and he threw in minimal mooring fees, which was pretty generous. We now had our very own boat in front of home and office. Our enthusiasm was firing on all cylinders now and on a trip to Miami, we kitted up on VHF radio, aerial, fishing rods, tackle and sundry other items including life jackets, snorkelling gear, in fact the whole caboodle.

Now admittedly to start with I had the somewhat naïve notion that boats simply sat in the water, involved no work and were cheap to run. You readers who are boaters are probably just about picking yourselves off the floor about now with laughter having read this gobbledygook. Anyway on the following Sunday it was our maiden voyage on The Ship of Fools (well actually it didn't have a name, although potentially it could have been the "Titanic Junior' given the idiots at the controls).

We got off to an inauspicious start, the engine fired up bubbling away at the back, but nothing happened as we forgot to untie all of the mooring lines. Dilemma solved we ventured across the marina to the fuelling depot run by a very amiable diver Quint Riskit (who ran the only diving operation at that time and a great guy to know). We filled up and I couldn't believe the cost , it was at the fair rate, but I thought boats were like cars. I didn't quite have to pawn our possessions but it took all our available cash. You almost expected the boat to burp with satisfaction at its complete intake.

Then it was out down the channel leading to the sea. You

will remember that scene in Jaws when they are taking the boat out to catch the shark and it is viewed through a pair of sharks hanging jaws as it ominously heads out into the unknown. Well that was us, although being British we did have a picnic on board as opposed to rifles and spear guns

Outside the channel was the expanse of water within the reef. Still vast but what was quite scary was the sheer clarity of the water. You could see the sandy bottom and also the great sinister rocks that seemed to surge towards you as you plodded along undulating with the waves, exaggerated on account of the light refraction. You had to stick to the marked and staked route, with red and green posts guiding you at about quarter mile intervals.

As you steered away from the beach looking back it was just spectacular and gave you a completely different perspective of the island. The air was brisk and sporadically spray hit you in the face as the boat plunged onwards. The sky was a brilliant light blue and the sun beamed down with warmth. I realised what it was that made devotees to the boating life. So far so good.

We motored eastwards toward Leeward at the Island's extremity and looking to the reef out further by some half a mile I noticed the spectacular crashing of the waves over the rocks just submerged below. Then I spotted Sellars Cut, the break into the ocean beyond. I just had to go there, Hemingway's Old Man and the Seas stuff, totally against my normal caution (lying again, fear being the word). The boat seemed to plunge more and we steered through the cut out into the ocean when everything became strangely calmer.

Then for some unknown reason the engine stopped. Help I thought, next stop Cape Cod! Panic started to surge, but after waiting a few minutes and trying the starter again, it kicked to life. Relief! Hurriedly we headed back into the reef but somehow I had misplaced my bearing and large spikey rocks loomed dangerously up to us below the boat. One struck the boat so I retreated back into the ocean again. Calmer I realised the gap lay a little more to the east and we bolted through it. Phew! Still in one piece.

We stayed within the reef after that and motored way eastwards, past Little Water Cay, Pine Cay, where the odd person on the beach would wave like a miniature insect distant. Just off Dellis Cay we moored about two hundred yards off the beach and tried snorkelling. The depth was about thirty feet and as you looked afar the sea appeared gloomy blue as if something might suddenly emerge out of the obscurity, not too alarming I hoped. I looked down and a six foot nurse shark (harmless) swam straight under me within about two feet. Before the Jaws theme music could begin we hopped back on board and set off again towards Parrot Cay.

We had gone some miles now from Turtle Cove. As we tore along suddenly I spotted a figure in my side vision behind and it was leaping out of the water continually following in our wake. This was none other than our National Treasure JoJo the dolphin. Arguably the most popular character in the Islands.

JoJo is a wild animal and you must always respect that fact, but at his own volition and when it suits him he will interact with humans, be they in boats or swimming near the shore. Dolphins do pass through the Island's waters but JoJo has made them his home and he rarely strays from them. He is extremely friendly and will let people touch him, but if he wants to be solitary he will let you know and you must respect that. He had been around some years when I first came and thankfully he still is at the time of writing, delighting us with his presence. This time he was using our wake as a sort of Jacuzzi and loving it, cackling in the way they do sometimes. They are very powerful and fast and on this occasion he sped ahead and actually leaped across our bow. Incredible stunt stuff. We were ecstatic. And then as suddenly as he appeared he was gone.

JoJo is actually protected by law and I think at some stage had been assigned a warden to look after his welfare. On one occasion some clot at Club Med upon meeting him stuck his finger over JoJo's blow hole. Understandably the poor animal reacted and barged the intimidating twit away. The imbecile then wanted to sue for distress. Impossible under our laws but presumably there were no end of ambulance chasing legal vultures in the U.S. who would try to pursue it. The truculent guest was quietly taken aside by the G.O's and advised that if he wanted to vacate the Islands in one piece, his better counsel would be to shut up. Nothing further transpired.

We headed back and just off Pine Cay we tried our fishing rods. Now neither of us had done this before and the bait was a sort of metal feathered spinning lure. The thing to do was to caste it as the boat sped along and to see what happened. We were not exactly at ease with hooking some unsuspecting fish and rather hoped nothing would result in this. I mean if you are happily about to take a bite out of a hamburger in Macdonalds only to find it has a large hook in it and you end up being reeled up to the counter, well it sort of sucks.

Then the line started jerking and the rod tip bending and we reeled in a little fish. Carefully we extracted the hook which thankfully had not done any apparent damage to it and we put it in the fishing well located in the centre of the boat. Feeling somewhat sorry for it we tried to extract it from the well, but it was so slippery we couldn't get a hold of it. Unwittingly we both tried our hands at this with the result that temporarily no one was steering the boat and it started going around in violent circles. We somehow got hold of it and it slipped out of our grip and plopped thankfully back into the ocean, hopefully none the worse for its experience. I don't think Hemingway would have been proud of us.

Back on course we decided to moor just off Little Water Cay to have a late lunch with the picnic we had brought. Now there is an art in mooring a boat offshore from the beach. The general idea being to ensure that you are not swept by the surf onto the beach, so the anchoring is important. Well this disable seaman got it wrong and lo and behold the boat got swept up onto the beach and try as we did we could not dislodge it. I hadn't figured on my first trip out to have need of a May Day distress call, albeit from dry land, but that seemed to be the sum total of it. I tried the VHF but nothing seemed to respond, in fact the button on this machine had got stuck in the on position.

Let's put it this way, situations like this put stresses on any relationship and a heated discussion ensued along the lines of what another fine mess you've got me into . After about half an hour a boat approached us and it was an American friend, Karl Lifeliner, the sort of quiet guy whose actions were louder than his words and just the type you need when you were in a fix like this. He got us towed back in the water with ease and then in his discreet inimitable way suggested boats and me were not the best of mixes.

True to the unspoken law of mariners he would take no payment and that really summed up the sort of great guy he was. He had obviously heard our May Day call. Getting back to Turtle Cove and disembarking we ran into Hyram who enquired whether we had had an enjoyable day. "Oh yes, great" given in true Brit polite fashion somewhat falsely, but otherwise looking a bit like survivors off a raft.

Next morning and doing the rounds downtown, people kept coming up and asking whether we got back alright. Karl wasn't the only one listening to our plight and other rantings over the VHF!

Chapter 24

Bozo To Dog Baskets

Hyram met his match once and it was in the form of a parrot called Bozo. Bozo was a magnificent blue and yellow Macaw who resided out at the plant nursery newly established some miles away out at Leeward. He was something of a celebrity in his own right because although he spent most of the time there he would occasionally escape and venture off on adventures of his own.

His big pal at the nursery was a delightful character called Rummy Skinfull, a retired British guy who was in effect the manager. There wasn't always a lot to do in those days, so Rummy would sit in a wicker rocking chair gently imbibing in rum and coke, his favourite tipple. Rummy would keep the glass nearby readily at hand and Bozo, when Rummy fell asleep with his intake which was not infrequently, would tuck his beak in the glass and top up as well. So in effect you had an inebriated Rummy and Bozo in charge of the place. Not that anyone minded.

One Sunday afternoon I even found Rummy in his car downstairs in the car park. He was clearly out for the count and when I woke him up (as you wondered if anything serious might be wrong) he just sleepily indicated that he was simply dozing off the effects of an excellent lunch at the nearby restaurant. Later the car was gone and really that summed up Provo in those days, people sort of kept an eye on one another and there was an air of tolerance to life. Now we are more cosmopolitan!

I was waiting in my office one morning as Hyram wanted to see me on something. He was always on time and I still had about twenty minutes before his arrival. My main office had a splendid two sided view of the marina and the sun shone in very pleasantly and yet without dazzling you. From that there was a long corridor to the front door with minor rooms to the side. Either side of the door were wooden louvred windows, very effective for letting the breeze through.

Suddenly there came what sounded like an intense scratching at one of the louvred panels and upon going to see I could make out a narrow face and beak grabbing at the panel and actually munching away at it. It was Bozo and his beak was like a pneumatic drill, chipping furiously away at the splintered wood and what was fast becoming a shattered panel. I shouted and he must have taken flight as I heard a sort of wafting of wings.

More to the point what would Hyram make of it, as he had an eagles eye for detail; especially his own property. As fate would have it, some minutes later he entered and came lumbering down the corridor, a bit like a prize fighter approaching the ring, he came into my main office. Had I ever seen anything like it, to which I replied nope. Any idea what it was? Here comes the tricky part as I didn't want to land my little blue and yellow friend in the proverbial. I toyed with the idea of suggesting the cause being some turbo charged termites, but thought better of it as it did sound a bit crass in the circumstances. Surprisingly I managed to change the topic of conversation as I deflected attention on to his favourite topic, business.

We must have been chatting for about half an hour or so when Hyram stopped and had a look of profound horror on his face, he had spotted a sign displayed on the side cabinet. I better explain. I had in fact picked it up in Miami when shopping and frankly couldn't resist it. The idea I think came from Michener's novel 'Centennial'. There one of his characters upon entering a lawyers office for advice found the counsellor tapping an identical sign right in front of his desk before anything commenced. It read "All a lawyer has to sell are his knowledge and his time and they are as precious to him as goods are to a tradesman." Now as far as I was concerned this was just a bit of fun and I even had another sign on my door saying "No Soliciting".

As I indicated before Hyram was not one for laughing. He asked what my hourly rate was (and I decided no more joking) and told him. It was as if a three hundred and fifty pound ball had just been shot from the mouth of a cannon. The conversation ended abruptly (he had just remembered something that had to be done urgently) and he barrelled down the corridor. Not forgetting to open the door, as it was his; as he could easily have propelled himself straight through it. End of session. Or so I thought.

There then came an almighty roar; Hyram's of course. I went down the corridor and peered out through the front door and took in the sight that greeted me looking down the passageway outside. There a few doors along, completing his programme of drilling, was Bozo waddling along attacking the last of the louvred windows. Outside each shattered window lay piles of splintered wood.

Hyram was dumbstruck and when he did spring into action it was too late. Bozo was safe high up in a tree, his head bobbing up and down and cackling away. Doubtless Hyram had visions of what roasted parrot on a spit looked like. Now Bozo, unlike the cockatoo Birdie in Grand Turk, was polite and in fact all the expletives were coming from Hyram. Bozo eventually flew off, presumably to one of his safe sanctuaries.

One of those sanctuaries belonged to Crazy Sam. He had a sort of junk yard on the south side of Provo because quite simply he never threw anything away (a bit like Sandford & Son or Steptoe and Son's backyards). He wasn't a hoarding nutter, it's just that he found a use for everything he had. It just took time. Sam was an old hand and time did not merit the same neurotic deference most modern people today have or more accurately suffer from. He actually had a heart of gold and what he didn't know about boats was not worth knowing or more to the point he had forgotten more than any other person did know.

He was average size with piercing blue eyes, probably in his mid fifties then, and with a vast mop of unkempt wavy hair. He relished in island living and the simplicity it afforded in those days. He was extremely able and always willing to lend a hand to anyone in need. He had originally been a technician when the old Pan Am base had been functional in Grand Turk.

His skill with boats was so renowned that often when very expensive yachts had been built (and we are talking about millions of dollars worth here) the owners would entrust Sam to deliver the yachts wherever they were required, often quite far afield. He was to be trusted and with good reason. He also had a wonderfully succinct gift for summing situations up. For example, when some lunatic of a youngster once took a valuable boat and crashed it on the reef, Sam's only reaction, in typical technical parlance was "He's wired up all wrong".

He tended to hang out with an equally affable friend of his called Welly. Welly looked a bit similar although somewhat smarter. He was a relative of one of the founding Seven Dwarves who instigated so much in Provo. He was obviously a man of substance, but typical of his character he had no need to show it and he was held in widespread respect. The two of them would often drive around in a pickup truck.

I remember on one occasion a friend of mine pointed to the rear of their truck as they left a store. There were three of them, Sam, the dog (a scruffy golden retriever) and Welly all seated together and from behind, through the window, they had identical hair profiles, so you couldn't tell who was who. Most significantly, all animals adored both Sam and Welly; always a good sign. Bozo had a safe refuge there.

As it turned out my escapades with animals were far from over for that day. In the evening we were to dine with Kaiser Von Riechthofen and his friends at his residence, located high up (well high by Provo standards) on a hilly area called Blue Mountain, on the northern side and sort of in the middle of the Island. Kaiser was a resplendent individual. German as you can guess but with English, especially elocution, spoken to perfection. In fact that's how you could tell he wasn't English, he spoke it too well, and without any hint of an accent. He was highly educated, a splendid soft spoken voice (in fact he was an excellent tenor singer as well) and with a very English and funny sense of humour. To look at him he closely resembled the actor Dirk Bogarde and many of the girls were quite taken with him. He owned and ran an art gallery in the mid part of town, in fact in a very colonial styled and attractive development. His parents were delightful and

I can recount many happy evenings spent in their company.

On this occasion he had invited our very eminent historian Curtis Lemar and others were present. I particularly remember two of his newer acquaintances, a father and son, called Oliver and Horatio Beeslop. Both highly erudite in their own right and teachers at a local school. As usual the evening went well with the hosts excelling themselves. As part of the main course we had some Cornish hens which were delicious but they were stuffed to the gunnels with garlic. Noddy Cowslip, another English guest, simply mentioned with admirably polite observation and understatement "I detect a tinge of garlic in this".

The wine of course flowed. Probably causal on account of this were Curtis and Oliver (who had really hit it off intellectually so to speak) finding a mutual interest in medieval Italian poetry and deciding to conduct their reflections on the subject in latin. At least that was my memory of events. Well, this wasn't exactly my area of comfort and conversations having hived off into topics such as decorating and gardening elsewhere, I took my temporary leave, having replenished my wine glass, and went outside on to the deck to take in the fresh air.

I sat down, albeit a bit low I thought, on a very comfortable chair with basket sides and promptly nodded off. I awoke suddenly with what seemed wet rubber duck on my nose followed by a large and very wet tongue slurping at my face. It was Sheba, their very friendly white German Shepherd. I had had the temerity to occupy her bed!

Kaiser also hosted very enjoyable art shows from time to time as his specialty was Haitian art, which was very popular and we bought several attractive pieces over the years. The colour and imagination really hits you. These are invariably gifted people painting under conditions of extreme poverty and it's nice to see them able to improve their lives in this way with the monies earned.

Apart from splendid nibbles Kaiser had a secret rum punch recipe, which frankly remained unsurpassed in my view. The punch bowl levels declined dramatically during these events. You could never get Kaiser to divulge the recipe and it took the format of a sacred secret pledge with it only being passed on to its family successor as the last act of the outgoing keeper of this sacrament. All a joke of course, but much fun was had in those days.

Chapter 25

Momentous Events

In the early nineties there were three events which occurred in Provo and which had quite a dramatic impact on everyone's lives here. The first was the opening of the Ramada Hotel in 1990. It was probably one of the most aesthetically pleasing hotels I have ever seen in the West Indies as it was entirely in character. If you imagine a large old style colonial home in the Florida Cays and simply enormously enlarge it, that just about represents what we got.

The architect was a talented British guy called Nick Weathervane. It had large louvred coverings to the windows (even Bozo couldn't make an impact on those) and it had an expansive entrance with the reception just discreetly to the side. The view as you went in took your breath away because the whole place opened up so that you saw right through to an enormous pool, the sea and blue sky. Nothing to obstruct this.

Shops were placed along the sides with a casino discreetly descending to the right. Either side of the broad vista that greeted you there were open staircases leading to large conference rooms at the side. But on this upper floor pride of place went to a large nightclub/dancing floor and bar in one big room to the right and to the left a very tastefully designed restaurant. The whole point being that there was nothing claustrophobic about the place. You felt good simply by being in it.

Its location was some miles along from Turtle Cove where we were. Actually by road you went east along the main arterial road, the Leeward Highway, and where it turned left towards the sea and at an eventual right turn to Club Med it faced you as you approached that right hand turn. Very imposing. On one occasion I walked from Turtle Cove to Ramada along the beach, just miles of curving beach with just the Island Princess Hotel, Le Deck (a delightful small hotel) and nothing else (save for the odd property set well back from the beach). After about five miles you came to Ramada and after that there was really just Club Med about a mile further on and next to that a resort called Casalmara. I mention all of this because today the magnificent beach it fronted is almost cheek to jowl with modern but splendid condo/hotels and resorts.

Ramada had a huge impact on the social life of Provo in those days. It was somewhere else exciting to go. Of course there was Club Med. Once you were logged in and ticketed. But with Ramada you could go in and out just as you pleased; whether it be shopping, dining, having a drink or simply taking in the atmosphere of the place.

They only made one inexplicable gaff. For some bizarre reason they decided to place a small table in the very front when you went through the entrance. On it they displayed a very yellow waxy looking effigy of a tourist. Male I think decked out in small shorts that had expired in style back in the seventies and seemingly stretching upwards as if trying to reach a beach ball in flight. It epitomized a tacky looking tourist, the only item missing being a knotted handkerchief on its head, but no one ever seemed to complain and so it endured.

The second tumultuous event and a great boon for the future tourist industry was the arrival of American Airlines and their scheduled service. It took up the void left by the sad demise of Pan Am. True we had to come up with a quarter of million dollar guarantee for the airline, but that proved a sound investment as it sprouted so many more to the plethora of air services we get today.

In the interim period we had survived by courtesy of other airlines adding extensions to their schedules, such as Cayman Airways and Carnival to name a few. These were vital lifelines which in effect kept our tourist industry on life support as it were.

One airline flew a DC10 into Provo Airport with passengers. Although it landed with just enough runway, trouble was they hadn't figured out the difficulties of taking off again and the normal complement of passengers had to be left and catered for by another flight. Otherwise it wouldn't have gotten off the ground.

They also encountered another problem altogether when they initially landed and tried to disembark their passengers. I actually witnessed this when driving down to the airport. The plane was so big and the doors so high up the airport didn't have moveable stairs high enough for the passengers to disembark. The highest set they had came about four feet too short of the door. So for the next three hours staff assisted each passenger from the aircraft bridging the gap to the moveable stair; cabin crews lifting each passenger to the ground staff at the top of the staircase. Heaven knows what results a passenger survey would have produced about journey satisfaction afterwards. Needless to say there was never any repetition of this flight.

As to the third momentous event I now become somewhat

hesitant (explanation forthcoming). The opening of the Golf Course. Of course (sorry for the pun) it was a tremendous facility and again added to the tourist dimension of our economy. It was wholly owned and funded by the ruling family of the Middle Eastern State of Qatar and they had an extremely able retired attorney who drove the whole project with verve and panache. It was a great success.

As a preliminary, they sensibly developed a water making plant and facility (golf courses tend to be thirsty) and this also became the central supply system for the entire Island. The course itself was to a high design; I think by a famous American designer called Kyle Litton. Everything was done to perfection. Now to me and the subject of golf in itself.

Was it Mark Twain who once said "golf is a nice walk spoilt." I know this is positively sacrilegious and blasphemy to golfing aficionados. Don't get me wrong, I love watching the pros on television; it has such a delightful technical expertise and seeming calm to it. They must have the patience of saints or is it really internal turmoil wonderfully disguised.

Unfortunately when I play I discover personality traits I would rather not know about. Rather the bad tempered Donald Duck of desk assembly fame. In short, I have no aptitude for the game and I am stupid enough to continue when upon doing the rare half decent shot I forget about the vast portion of veritable disasters. Actually I could probably merit an entire column in the magazine "Farmers Weekly", in the ploughing section! Completely infra dig, I have even managed to play another golfers ball (serious golfers get so worked up over such trifles!). Once in desperation I threw the club high into the air in frustration, not realizing it was heading for the cart which had my spouse sitting in it. Immediate panic ensued. Luckily it missed and there was a roof on it. But actually its fellow players that can be even more interesting, which brings to mind two other characters previously appearing in this story.

Rob Clarkwallis (of North Caicos fame) liked to play golf, having previously aspired at the game at the Burnley Municipal Golf Course, where else but in Burnley UK; a northern industrial town where rain and wind were the norm. He was actually a good player, but being a surveyor, the hunting out instinct was in his DNA and he would forever be looking out for other lost golf balls in the bushes when retrieving his own misplaced ball.

He sometimes took an age in these feverish searches. This spawned no good will at all with parties following up behind and you could sometimes feel the waves of hate coming at you as you pathetically tried to gesticulate what was going on. But Rob was a relative golfing lightweight compared to the other old timer who liked to play golf, being none other than Hank Puddinbasin of Parrot Cay fame, alluded to earlier.

Hank was arguably the most relaxed person I have ever met. Golf suited him mentally. You often hear about the sheer anxt that consumes nervous and anxious golfers when addressing the ball. Concentration personified. There is that wonderful description of such a golfer by P.G. Wodehouse, upon addressing the ball at tee off "he found the noise of the butterflies in the adjoining meadow positively deafening". Hank must have been into his late maturity then and was proud to be a 'Floridian Redneck'.

He was quite tall, at least six feet. He had a weather beaten face with trench like lines and was very tanned having spent his entire life outdoors. It was as if he had taken a long lease on his face and had grown so used to it he simply couldn't be bothered to move out. He had an utterly mischievous twinkle in his eyes and was always looking for a prank; a thoroughly nice guy, but invariably at someone else's expense.

He had an absolute mop of straight hair, quite thick but neatly trimmed at the extremities; really as if when having it cut (probably once every six months) the barber simply put a pudding basin over his head to achieve the long standing and desired effect. He was a sort of septagenerian Huck Finn and unorthodox in everything he did. His wife once told me he ate chicken to which I simply replied "that's nice". "But every day and for every meal!" she retorted. You couldn't help but like him. There was a function once and someone offered to bring him a drink from the bar. His favourite tipple being strong dark rum with just a tinge of Coca Cola. He got just a glass of the latter. Taking a sip I will never forget his expression. "What Goddam stuff is this" he looked aghast. You would think he had just ingested cyanide.

He was actually one of the original Seven Dwarfs landing on Provo and his designated role was as joker, which you could well understand. He was an ace golfer and could, at one time, have played the game professionally. He could hit the ball long and straight, often better than many of his younger members at the Club.

Coaching though was not his forte although playing a joke was. A quick illustration. When the Club opened, potential members and beginners, including yours truly, were invited for coaching demonstrations. We had the golf pro, a very nice and experienced guy , who took one group (as there were quite a few of us) and Hank who took the other group. We were all at the driving range in one long line hitting shots. I happened to be in Hanks line.

On addressing the ball he suggested we each stand with our legs as far apart as possible and swing at the ball, with the result that most of us landed up on the ground. Hank had a wicked grin on his face. The golf pro students of course received a more conventional education on the subject and were left standing. The Pro looked bewildered at the seeming carnage going on in the other line.

Now in stark contrast to this, one day Hank and another friend of ours Stan (he was a good player, but perpetually played with a cigarette alight in his mouth, save when teeing off when it dropped out of his mouth to the ground), at the suggestion of Hank we all played together. I simply could not stop laughing at Hank's antics and believe it or not did the best nine holes I ever did and by far. Relaxation.

Hank would often hook up with tourists from Club Med. who liked to play. Each session had a familiar pattern. Hank would start off playing perhaps the first nine holes in a very mediocre fashion. Then he would suggest a small wager with the visitor over the remaining nine holes, the outcome being that the loser would buy lunch and drinks. The hapless victim upon agreeing (thinking the outcome a sure thing) would suddenly see Hank's game spring to life and with devastating winning effect. Hank hardly ever had to pay for lunch.

He came a bit unstuck once though. Hank had had prostrate problems and consequently surgery had left him with a degree of discomfort when playing. Having difficulty addressing the ball the visitor politely asked what the problem was. Hank not wanting to go into detail said "it's my feet". "Oh, that's interesting" said the visitor "I happen to be a doctor and a specialist in feet, what's the problem?" Hank retorted "I keep peeing on them"!

For my part, perhaps I should have followed Groucho Marx's maxim, when contemplating membership of the Golf Club: "I would never want to be a member of any club that wanted me as a member." Actually they did excel themselves as far as I was concerned every Christmas by holding a stupendous party which went with a bang, much like my game of golf! There endeth the lesson on golf thankfully.

A sad epilogue to Ramada. It went through further ownership and closed. It was demolished many years ago, much to the disappointment of us all.

Chapter 26

A Question of Security, Panama Jack and 007

Having been resident in the Islands some five years now, it seemed only fitting for us to try to upgrade our status there. Up to that point we had to obtain a yearly work permit renewable annually at Government's discretion. Don't get me wrong on this, it had always been renewed without fuss (actually it's one of the crowning features of the Islands when seeking to attract investment). But clearly if you were investing your future there you needed something more substantial in terms of security.

As alluded to before, there was a provision in the law that made this feasible for suitable professionals, so that was the elected route and we thought it a good idea (given our time spent in Grand Turk) to personally take the applications over there and hand them to the Chief Minister ourselves, as that area of responsibility fell within his portfolio.

It's funny when you go back to a place; in fact we hadn't been back to Grand Turk in over two years. Small communities are always different with certain factors often somewhat heightened. Strangely enough you tended to feel a bit of a betrayal factor for leaving. It's never a nice feeling having left people behind, although you dealt with the same people every day by telephone in a perfectly cordial manner. I should add that subsequently we went back more frequently. Would it by like a stranger wandering through some Mid-West American small town with waves of resentment projected at him. Especially given the Grand Turk/ Provo antipathy previously alluded to. Not a bit of it as it turned out. As we went down Front Street to the Chief Minister's Office several people we knew came up and asked after our well being.

The only slight hitch lay at the Chief Minister's Office. Although we had lived in Grand Turk he was oddly enough one of the very few we did not know in any true sense of the word. This was "Hoppy", who had been elected to office straight after the Commissions of Enquiry. He was very pleasant. To look at he was of a compact medium build; in fact I could well imagine him making out as a reasonable welter weight boxer.

But his opener was a knock out punch. "You've got two things against yer" he growled. "You're white and you're in Provo". I asked him whether he would like us to hand the applications to Miss. Shredder outside his office and be done with it. Momentarily regretting it, since this was perhaps not the best time for an attempt at humour. But he sat back in an enormously well upholstered swinging chair put his hands together, stuck a large sausage like finger in our direction and said "I will make enquiries and you will hear from me". Maybe not so bad as it seemed after all.

The fellow was as good as his word and we actually received our Certificates about a year and a half later. You have to bear in mind that these sort of things were not handed out with any degree of frequency then. Today there must be something, although guessing, in the region of two thousand issued. I am pretty sure our old friend in Immigration, Wally Longbourne, would have been one of Hoppy's checks and he had actually encouraged us to apply! It says a lot for the place and of him, actually both of them. The time factor wasn't so bad either.

Things do unintentionally get misplaced at times. I know of one deserving lady who, not having heard for over a year on her application, went across to Immigration in Grand Turk from Provo to enquire about it's progress. She was speaking to an official and suddenly noticed that a bundle of papers were serving as a rather wet coaster to a plant pot. It turned out it was her very own application. The ensuing embarrassment did cause things to happen I was told.

We later got naturalized and obtained Belongership status (conferring the full set of rights bestowed upon any citizen of the Islands), again without problems. This gave complete security. On the last Certificate issued, called Belongership, the Governor's Office had misplaced them and Wally spent a whole afternoon chasing them down and when he did so he sent them over by Federal Express to Provo with "Congratulations" inscribed on the envelope. The Head of Immigration doing that. This was some friend indeed!

Not long after the Grand Turk trip we received a visit from another client who had wanted to visit and set up a company and bank account for an overseas business. Freddie Floggit was no run of the mill U.K. style of Brit. He was a very nice person to deal with but his antics sometimes, well, could be termed a bit bizarre. Freddie had made it up the hard way, he had been brought up in an orphanage but had gone on to become immensely successful (as to what in, I will come to in a minute).

He had impeccable introductions from eminent Swiss and London law firms and had a partner (not with him on the visit to the Islands) called Reginald Ribald-Chumley. Reggie was in total contrast to Freddie, public school (private school, to our North American friends) and Sandhurst Military College.

Reggie looked like Captain Kirk in Star Trek and as for Freddie, well, he could have been running a jellied eel pie stall in the East End of London, which is where he came from. He just had a pleasant countenance to him and you could imagine him shouting out special prices to his customers.

Freddie had company with him on this trip. He had somehow made contact with an old friend he hadn't seen since his orphanage days, Cyril Blastout. Cyril lived in Atlanta, where he had gone on to be successful in an exporting business if I recall correctly.

Freddie's female accompaniment was something else altogether. He had hired a girl from a high class escort service in Mayfair, London called Veronica Plimley-Smythe, solely for this trip; she looked and sounded like a debutante and she told us that she had attended the prestigious Rhodean Private Girls School in England. But nothing redolent of the lacrosse or hockey fields in this lady. Very attractive, voluptuous you might say, long wavy hair (the sort you get on hairspray lacquer cans). She wore the shortest of skirts possible and to elevate the effect sat on a pod stool in the bar where we first met them (in the Hotel just above Turtle Cove, the Erebus as it was called then). She was no shrinking violet either and took an instant dislike to Freddie's friend Cyril over dinner. We tried to referee, but to no visible effect. In the end both stomped off to their rooms leaving us with Freddie to make plans for the ensuing day, which would be a visit to the Bank.

It was arranged that I would collect Freddie the next morning and drive him to the Bank. At this juncture I had better explain Freddie and Reggie's business. They had at one time lucrative contracts with the U.K. Government's Ministry of Defense. This was on the armaments side of things. So they were the good guys if I may gesture as much. But such were the vicissitudes of that industry they were now looking for completely fresh new ventures and they sort of hit it on the head early in those days, because they were going into the supply of drinking water from renowned spa sources.

Waiting outside the hotel for Freddie I got the shock of my life when he came out. He was dressed in a pure white suit, black shirt, white tie, bright white and black toned brogue shoes and a pure white Panama hat (actually made in Ecuador, as a bit of useless extra information). To top it he had dark black sunglasses. In short, I was taking Panama Jack to meet the Bank Manager. Del Boy of 'Only Fools and Horses' fame would have considered him real naff.

On the way down he apologized for his guests bahaviour, which clearly hadn't effected us at all, but I suggested that there was no dating potential between Veronica and Cyril, to which he laughed. He explained that his steady girlfriend, Jasmine, was a Turkish hairdresser and had a salon in Walthamstow in London, but couldn't get away. She knew all about Veronica and was understanding!

When we got to the Bank, I realised that Freddie had reserved the best for last. If the Bank manager had any reaction to Freddie's appearance he certainly wasn't showing it. He was a very nice guy from Antigua and I am sure he was smiling with his eyes politely. Freddie's letters of introduction were spot on for the bank. However, Freddie, upon describing his business made an opening gambit with something like "me and my partner were in the arms business, but since no one seems to be killing anyone anymore, well we're looking at something different". Monty Python's nudge, nudge, wink, wink, could have played a part in this dialogue. I wanted the floor to open up and swallow me. The Manager seemed totally unphased.

When it came to leaving, and as they were travelling on to

the Far East, Freddie and Veronica gave us numerous postcards to post on their behalf. The addresses were certainly diverse and reflective of the type of society kept by each of them. Several of Freddie's cards had addresses like "Ernie Lightfingers C/o of Widnes Open Prison." As for Veronica, she must have known the full complement of Officers in the Grenadier Guards, such as "Captain Sebastian Ponsonby-Willows, Waterloo Barracks, London, S.W.1." to name but one.

That evening we were hosting a cocktail party ; at our new home, up on a hill and with views of Grace Bay. It was a beautiful vista giving sweeping views of the entire North Bay and its beach. It was a pleasant mixture of people and one in particular as it turned out was famous in a somewhat discreet sort of way.

We knew his daughter Onoria Glossop and he and his wife were visiting her over what was the Christmas period. Onoria was a very pleasant lady perhaps in her mid thirties then and she was somewhat of an academic; taking an interest in everything about the Islands. She had initially come to Grand Turk as a journalist with the local newspaper and had then gone on to buy a quaint lodging house fronting the beach called Guinip Lodge. Onoria then renovated the place and it served, very popularly as it turned out, as a lodging place for visitors to Grand Turk.

She then took quite some time off in England to qualify as a lawyer there and came back to the Islands and was duly admitted to practice law, having joined a prominent law firm. At this point in time I think Onoria had left and was doing translating services from Lugano (a very beautiful part of Switzerland with mountains and lakes in seemingly perfect proportion and with a Mediterranean climate) where her parents lived. Onoria had retained a home in Provo.

Her parents were both charming and fascinating; age wise I would guess in their late seventies then. The mother was a beautiful and radiant wealthy American heiress. Whilst her father was English and even then cut a very smart distinguished figure. He stood over six foot tall and was slim but had obviously been powerfully built at some stage of his life. He had extraordinary dark intelligent eyes but with a benign polite expression to him. He stood absolutely upright and sported a sort of humbug patterned and coloured blazer which seemed entirely in keeping with his bearing. Not ostentatious mark you, just discreetly smart and someone you somehow respected immediately you met him. Sir Roderick Glossop (he was ennobled, but would be the last person to impart to you that fact) had a remarkable background.

He heralded from Yorkshire in England, graduated at Oxford University and had joined the Royal Navy before the commencement of World War 2. He was assigned to Naval Intelligence and rose rapidly through the ranks to become a secret undercover operative dealing in amongst other things espionage. When France fell in 1940 he was responsible for helping allied airmen shot down to escape the Germans by formulating escape routes with the Resistance fighters.

I should add this is not information that would have been divulged from his own lips. Rather research I did after meeting someone who you somehow know has done something special but without actually telling you. He took extraordinary risks behind enemy lines. His immediate superior Officer was none other than Ian Fleming (of the James Bond books and movie fame) and it seems that when conjuring up his hero he modeled him on the very man standing in front of me.

After the war he entered Parliament in the U.K. and became a life long trusted friend of Prime Minister Margaret

Thatcher and it turned out that she sought his opinions on a range of matters at relevant times. Sir Roderick had by the time I met him retired to his beautiful home high up overlooking Lugano. His passion in life had been gardening and in fact he had assiduously cultivated an award winning Japanese Garden which was his pride and joy.

Something else always stuck in my mind from that encounter. He asked polite questions as if he was genuinely interested in you and never for once went on about himself. It brought to mind another Dr. Johnson quote 'You assess a man's worth by how he treats people who are of no importance to him'. Our ennobled spy scored high marks on that one.

Chapter 27

Confy

It would certainly be no misnomer to describe Confy Bravefart as unusual. In fact in someways downright eccentric might be a more accurate description of him. He stood not far short of six foot in height, of fairly lean stature, with perhaps the slightest hint of a stoop, as reading lay at the fundamental core of his existence and he had a manner of examining texts with a somewhat round shouldered posture. He wore quite thick spectacles giving a slight hint of Mr. McGoo to him as long vision was sometimes prone to give him problems.

Although it won't mean much to our non UK friends, there was a very popular comedy in the U.K. years ago called "Rising Damp" and its star, called Rigsby, amounted to a near perfect depiction of Confy in terms of appearance and mannerisms (Rigsby was actually a penny pinching landlord of bedsits and forever making forlorn passes at his female tenants). Confy was actually a very good friend and was in fact possessed of a kindly disposition.

His curricula vitae was succinct. A first at Cambridge in law and top of his professional examinations. He simply loved the subject of law. It was neither his habit nor inclination to advertise himself. If you dealt with him professionally you rapidly became aware of his brilliance. He was one of the smartest lawyers I have ever come across. Confy also had the pronounced skill of interpretation and could explain complicated matters in simple terms with solutions, which whilst many lawyers think they have that skill, in truth not many do. He had that priceless fusion of the academic, practical and commercial. He was also great fun to deal with.

Confy came to the Islands, Grand Turk in fact, in the latter part of the Eighties. He joined one of the largest legal practices there. Actually it was something of a sinecure for him as he had only recently retired as head legal counsel and company secretary to one of the largest international chemical companies (FIZZO) (being based in Brussels but travelling the world), after some twenty years. In short he needed something to do and in Grand Turk with its casual bizarre lifestyle he had found a place that suited him down to a tee. At one stage he had even invested in the Turks Head Inn; certainly being no ardent follower of the temperance movement himself.

He had a penchant for the ladies, who perceived a mischievous kindness in him, and they had only to flutter their eyelids at him when in some dilemma and he would be doing pro bono (free) work for them, although he probably had payment in mind of another kind. There always seemed to be a bevy of them needing his assistance.

Confy had had a colourful existence at Cambridge where he had been a Boxing Blue. In one contest between the University and Sandhurst, at the famous military academy, the proceedings were presided over by none other than Field Marshal Bernard Montgomery of El Alamein fame who was to present prizes to the victors in the tournament. In those days Confy sported long hair and chose for the occasion the most startling set of extra long red and white striped boxing shorts. Confy duly won and upon being presented to the somewhat conservative Field Marshall was heard him to utter "My God what is the world coming to, we would never have won the war with this sort of specimen under my command." Confy was unphased.

His sporting prowess didn't end there as he also won cups for diving (not into the plentiful pubs and bars in Cambridge which he frequented). He actually knew Stephen Hawking the world famous physicist and often drank coffee with him in the Copper Kettle coffee shop there. Those were in Hawking's better days health wise.

Confy had an artistic faculty to his talents; having been taught the violin at public (private again) school he continued as an accomplished performer there. He could even have been a caricature of Sherlock Holmes. But it was his humorous traits that probably got him more deserved recognition and he was certainly one for a good prank. In fact he probably should have immersed himself in the renowned 'Cambridge Footlights Club" which spawned such famous contemporaries as John Cleese and Peter Cooke. Anyway you get the sort of personality we are into here.

His tastes in the Islands were simple and he was certainly never given to any sort of ostentation. Confy had a refreshing candor about him and never really saw the need for secrecy or, embarrassingly as it turned out sometimes, discretion.

Confy could display a delightful absent mindedness in certain situations. He had a flair for property renovation and development and on one occasion needed some gravel for a driveway. He knew the place to order this was somewhere along the South Dock Road in the industrial area of the Provo.

He duly went there and turned into the driveway of a compound with a large structure, only to be confronted by an enormous security guard, who stood in front of his car blocking any further progress into the place. There ensued furious protestations from Confy ranging from "get out of the way" to "my constitutional rights", but the guard wouldn't budge. Eventually one of them had the presence of mind to bring up the reason for Confy's presence there, it was the Guard. Confy wouldn't answer and demanded to get in. "But Sir, no one like you visits here, this is the Illegal Haitian Refugee Detention Centre." The gravel place was next door.

Sometimes his office antics fared no better. On one occasion he was demonstrating to a young local trainee lawyer in their offices in Grand Turk, how certain types of accounts were set out. He chose a hypothetical name for the client "A. Hitler Client Account". Perhaps not the best of choices. The hapless youngster duly rang Confy "Excuse me Mr. Bravefart, is Mr. Hitler an actual client of the firm?"

Confy liked to smoke and another time he was deeply engrossed in a telephone conversation with a lawyer overseas. He had the absent minded habit of discharging ash anywhere and often lit stubs into his waste bin. Suddenly Confi's attention was drawn to surging flames coming out of his waste bin. "You will have to excuse me" he said to the lawyer "I will have to get back to you, my office is on fire."

One morning one of his partners introduced a distinguished lady client to him in his office. The usual smoke made the atmosphere dense but upon shaking hands a thunderous noise emanated from a certain part of Confy's anatomy and strangely continued. It was almost as if the action of the shaking of hands was causing the loud discharge to continue and augment. The lady blushed but Confy continued as if nothing was amiss.

In some ways he was our answer to renaissance man. He spoke five languages fluently and had an ability at painting, cartoons and even slogans or perhaps more aptly described as graffiti. I remember one advertising a conference on "Schizophrenia" and then adding "I've half a mind to attend" and "Raquel Welch is effeminate." His real forte though was for Limericks and whilst they were wittily constructed and clever, they inevitably degenerated into the ribald and quite frankly needed censoring. You couldn't let him loose on just anyone; particularly ladies with their sensibilities.

His relationship with cars was curious and his adventures reminded me of those of "Toad" in "The Wind In The Willows". He must have gone through a few cars in his time. A few years ago we had a bad storm one night and the rain was torrential and caused a lot of flooding. The next day Confy was due to pay me a visit to discuss some work we were doing together. There were two routes to my office. The first and most preferable was the main Leeward Highway and the second was a back route which had large and at times deep pot holes. I remember cautioning him about it and suggesting the safer route. Cellphones were in their infancy then but it was fortunate he had one. I received a call and Confy said he had a slight problem. He had taken the dodgy route and I duly went round there to see what had happened.

I turned a bend in the road and about fifty metres ahead of me there was Confy in his car slap bang in the centre of a very water full pothole. The water had exceeded the height of the hood (bonnet) and inside the water level reached as high as Confy's chest, he being seated there just static with a newly lit cigarette in his mouth. This was a serious towing job and I didn't have a tow rope. Luckily I got hold of Rob Clarkwallis, who lived not far, who did have one plus a very powerful V8 pickup truck ideal for towing.

I was on one side of the pond, as you could fittingly call it, and when Rob arrived he was on the other side. But instead of immediately setting up the tackle for the tow job Rob got his camera out and wanted to take pictures (Rob was a keen and actually excellent photographer) of Confy and the car for posterity's sake.

By this time Confy had emerged from the car still chest deep in water and in response to Rob's callings for Confy to model for the situation, I don't think I have ever heard such a string of expletives in all my life coming from Confy. Like "what the...........does that ....think he's doing" and otherwise questioning Rob's parentage. Rob pulled him out, Confy eventually dried out and the car was a write off. Now's here's the real nub of it. Confy did exactly the same thing, in the same pot hole, two years later!

He was the perfect antidote for people with arrogant and bigoted attitudes. During his Cambridge days Confy would go home to his mother's at Cookham, a delightful riverside location in the affluent Thames Valley where she ran an antiques shop. Whilst his mother attended to buying items for the shop, its day to day running was entrusted to a somewhat pompous lady with distinct views on class and placement in society; a prude would be an understatement.

She had a daughter brought up in the best of traditions as her mother perceived. She did not know Confy well, so as a lark he dressed up one day as a native of India with white linen attire, turban, sandals and having blackened his appearance with dark shoe polish all over. He presented himself to the lady at the antique shop feigning interest in antiques much to a look of horror and disdain on her part.

Then came the real punchline, he had met her daughter and wanted her mothers permission to court her in the best traditions of his own upbringing; his caste being most acceptable in Southall. The woman nearly had an apoplectic fit on the spot. He was mimicking a sort of Peter Seller's take off of the accent. "Where do you come from" said the woman in panic, desperately trying to put off the ardent suitor's intentions, "Oh, me from Deli" Confy retorted. "New Delhi?" she bleated. "No, no, no, deli on the High Street in Slough."

Back within a professional context in Provo, Confy worked as a consultant for us and to great effect. On one occasion I had a matter right down his street. It was a complexed banking and financing transaction and I found myself dealing with a partner in one of the big San Francisco law practices. A very able guy indeed. Confy did the work and had to render an opinion, which I had to sign off on. The lawyer rang me up afterwards saying how pleased he was and that he considered the opinion one of the best he had ever come across. Politely, he expressed the view that he was just surprised that it came from a lawyer in Provo.

I promptly corrected him and said that his praise should go to Confy and the lawyer said would I mind if he spoke with him. Of course not was my response. The lawyer rang me the day after and said what a remarkable person Confy was and how illuminating the experience had been. He had him on the phone for well over an hour and what a sense of humour he had. He laughed and said he wondered what he could put the time spent down as on his time sheet. "Prolonged encounters of the entertaining kind", I proffered.

Chapter 28

It's a Dogs Life

Although the Islands and its characters make up the rich pageant of life there, its animals also have a place in the scheme of things. You've already heard enough of donkeys, cattle, parrots and dolphins but dogs are the unsung heroes of the Islands as well as they are so close to us in our lives. In fact they know more about us than the other way around because quite simply they have little else to study all day.

Companionship is also a big feature in the people/dog equation. Even if you don't look for them they somehow find you, at least that was certainly my case. On that subject I encountered three entirely distinctive personalities and it's also worth noting and learning how they interact with the various people that crop up in life. Mysterious? Not really.

They basically study us in order to serve their own best interests and all in all they are very good at it. If you've never owned a basset hound in life you really don't know what you are missing. Mine was called Fred. A magnificent animal, white, black and brown colouring. He had been born in Dadeland Florida and had a pedigree as long as your arm. His kennel name allocated to him was "Big Boozer", probably a reflection on his ultimate owner. He could have been the original 'Hush Puppy".

People make an unerring error with bassets and that is to under estimate their noses. They are the biggest scenting dogs after bloodhounds and their noses will dominate and lead them wherever the compelling smell in question takes them; irrespective of loud commands, volcano explosions or nuclear bomb tests. They are simply oblivious to anything else going on around them Actually that's a lie, except food. For that reason they are capable of roaming for days on end without so much as a thought to where home is. It therefore followed that Fred found himself doing the rounds of exasperated owners not knowing what to do with him. You have to spend time with them and make a point of not letting them wander.

Food and comfy sofas play a big part in that panacea. Like their owner they tend to have a distinct lack of interest in healthy exercise and are quite happy to while the way the hours in snoozing and sheer idleness. His antics tend to remind me of my limited acting debut. The part of Idle Jack in the school pantomime; a part that required no acting ability on my part whatsoever. (The other role that I sadly saw no debut in was as first reserve broomstick in the Sorcerer's Apprentice). But this is all rather straying from the point again.

Temperamentally they are the most benign natured creatures on this planet. They are French in origin "bas" I think pertaining to low but their little legs are like pistons and when they want to they can move with astonishing speed. Especially when leaping up on to a sofa, some three feet off the ground. A sort of ill timed Fosbury Flop. They are also the perfect antidote to stress. I can recall getting stressed at work, as sometimes happens, and just gazing down between the desk at a mournful face, big floppy ears and soulful eyes as if to say "what's all the fuss about". It works!

They are eccentric little dogs and very stubborn (explains the French in him). If they don't want to go somewhere, forget it. Their feet are like ABS brakes and with their low trajectory off the ground, they know you haven't a hope of budging them an inch. They are also not that great as guard dogs and I am pretty sure any burglar would get a guided tour of our house if he were to be bribed with a bit of cheese. You see they just like everybody.

Guarding the refrigerator is another matter and they keep a constant vigilance for what might fall out of it or, if you are careless enough to leave the door open, you will see his rear portion with the front end fully immersed and chomping at some goodies within.

I first encountered him some time before I took him on as an owner. A group of us were sitting having a drink down at the Yacht Club, Turtle Cove one lunch time. The bar was across from the hotel rooms which in some cases the doors had been left open. Fred used to like to visit the kitchens there for any pickings which he usually did well at because the staff were fond of him.

He was wandering along and happened to enter one of the rooms and after about two minutes there followed a woman's shrill scream, wondering what had come into her room. Let's face it, it was only a basset hound. He could wander far because at that stage his home was unrestricted and about a mile away. In those days traffic wasn't the unmitigating nuisance which it is today either.

On another occasion, when we owned him, my wife was attending some function and talking to some ladies and one of them explained how the previous Sunday they had held a barbeque at home for a number of friends. Their day was livened up by the arrival of a friendly basset hound who stayed with them a few hours and managed to munch his way through five steaks. Under those circumstances you tend to wonder whether it's wise to admit ownership of the culprit. It was a rare occasion when he had managed to sneak off for one of his walkabouts.

He had other unforgettable foibles. When Fred wanted your attention he would paw at you. It was like being struck with a boxing glove with nails in. In the morning he would often find your socks before you could and run off and guard them in his great jaws with his paws covered over them for good measure, to make recovery virtually impossible without ripping them. When pressed for time it was patience testing of a saint. The trade off to secure their release being a piece of cheese as an offering and deemed adequate compensation. By that time well salivated socks were not exactly of any use.

Like all hounds he had the unique habit of baying. Not often, but when he did it started as a low wooing sound, deep and resonate, building to a crescendo and then lowering and undulating from then on and could continue for some time, as the mood took him. It was a bit eerie but rather wonderful to listen to.

Fred's wandering antics were somewhat curtailed by the arrival of a friend for him called Whiskey, a black and white border collie. Again she had somehow acquired us and hit it off immediately with Fred. They became inseparable. Strange really as there was a sort of stridency about them. Whiskey was the exact antithesis of Fred. Very quick and almost highly strung, but again with a loveable temperament.

Fred seemed less inclined to break out when Whiskey was around. However, she managed to nuzzle through gates, fences and was an expert tunneller. A sort of escape artist, Houdini if you like of the dog world. She could have featured in "The Great Escape. She always returned after an hour or so. Confy said he would have been truly impressed if she had managed to shore and board the tunnel up by way of support. They really are incredibly intelligent dogs.

Whiskey was also an expert sandwich thief. If you carelessly left one on the table, she would amble by and with one stroke of her tongue actually manage to swipe the contents out of the sandwich, leaving the bread which she didn't care for. I half expected to find diagrams of her plotted enterprises. As you can guess, Whiskey was an excellent guard dog. Their ears and noses are something like two hundred times stronger than our own senses.

On the rare occasion our intrepid duo broke out together. One of their escapades resulting in my receiving a phone call one late afternoon from the local liquor store some two miles away. The kindly proprietor was feeding them potato chips as they had just wandered by to see what was on offer. In some ways they were a lethal cocktail of chaos with their antics. Often the chaos that ensued reminded me of Sooty and Harry H. Corbett, a TV show very popular in the U.K. for many years. Sooty being a mischievous and uncontrollable little bear puppet and invariably the shows ended having degenerated into pure pandemonium with Harry their controller despairing at the mayhem created by Sooty with his pal Sweep a little dog puppet.

Our third dog Bingo was something else altogether and yet again he found us. He was an Island dog, a puppy in fact, who had been badly treated and abandoned. A restraining wire around one paw and a collar so tight it cut into the poor animal. From the first day he came around looking for food his salvation was assured.

Trouble was getting hold of him to get him treated. We have wonderful animal welfare organizations in the Islands (excellent vets as well) and a friend who was trying to get hold of Bingo said he must have administered enough knock out substance to bring a horse down. Anyway it worked and we had a healthy dog on our hands once fixed up.

The Island dogs are called Potcakes. They are the original dogs brought to the Islands and potcake derived from the habit of feeding them the residue of food left at the bottom of the pots once folks had eaten. They are smart loveable animals and are very popular. Many finding homes with visitors abroad.

In Bingo I sometimes think I have found the perfect case to defeat the Dog Whisperer. Alright, not seriously, but he has certain antics (games as far as he is concerned) which can have laughable results. I don't know whether you recall that wonderful American humourist James Thurber. There was a series about him called something like "My Life And Welcome To It". This was some years ago.

Well every time he came home from work, his dog (who positively adored the rest of his family) wouldn't let him through the front door. For some reason reminiscent of Fred Flintstone putting the sabre toothed tiger cat out for the night who then jumps through the window and puts Fred out on the doorstep instead, leaving him wailing for Wilma to let him back in. Actually I just love the excuse to recount that funny episode.

My situation is a bit different with Bingo. He won't let me out of the house. Every attempt to do so entails barking and ferocious snapping right up until you close the door from outside with the parting shot being the snapping jaws as the door slams shut. When anyone happens to visit at the same time and sees this spectacle of a disheveled shape escaping they end up in fits of laughter. And here's the real embarrassment to all this his tail is wagging with glee the whole time. My wife has no such trouble. So here is a plea to any readers out there with a plausible solution, short of strangling him, please spew forth with your advice.

Anyway, enough on the dog topic. I promised I would mention them and they would have been miffed if I hadn't. In truth they really do enrich your life and are great fun (except when trying to get out of the house!).

Chapter 29

And The World Turned Upside Down

That was the title to the tune played by the victorious Continental Army when they defeated the British at Yorktown during the American War of Independence. When the able General Cornwallis laid down his arms and along with his retinue marched out to that particular fanfare. It was a pivotal changing point in the war and change is what brought this subject to mind. The relevance here being the change to the Islands since the commencement of this missive some thirty-five years ago now.

The events and people captured represent a time capsule spanning some ten years, when the Islands were for the most part unchanged and I cannot see a replication of them ever happening again, which has made them so special. I have enjoyed being frivolous in my recounting of events, because quite simply they were enjoyable and stress free times, sadly lacking in today's world. Not to debase the Islands today in any way because they are still unique, but there needs to be an elaboration on factors which have impacted in common with just about everywhere in the Western World today. And in many ways the Islands are a microcosm of that world.

What I do want to refrain from here is getting into tedious political dogma (which is a pain), but more to illustrate the practical external forces which have impacted the Islands and caused them to lose a certain pristine unspoilt quality and carefree existence. There is also a sort of persistent nagging that goes on nowadays by the elitist and bureaucratic forces that seek to control our lives. So, as spoilers, they have sort of brought what follows on themselves.

Before another word is said, if you are contemplating visiting the Islands for a vacation, well don't hesitate. Make a booking and just come. It is a magnificent place for a holiday with a long beach consistently voted the best in the world with a plethora of wonderful resorts, villas and hostelries.

The supporting infrastructure is unbeatable with a hospitality industry second to none. Credit goes to a vast number of people who have worked their butts off to create a great product and the local government deservedly takes credit for this as well. Add to it that there are no restrictions on owning real estate; many people buy and build holiday homes.

What follows therefore should be construed within that context and is an observation upon how actual living conditions have changed throughout the world, which many regard as inevitable and some would even mark as progress.

Up until about twenty-five years ago the FCO (Foreign and Commonwealth Office), which is ultimately responsible for and controls its colonies (correction, Dependent Territories), including the Islands, took a somewhat laissez affaire approach to its charges. As previously indicated we represented something of an anachronism to them that they really didn't know what to do with.

As a consequence the Islands continued as a sort of one man and a dog operation outside the main flow of the worlds affairs and most things that arose could be dealt with by applying a little common sense and goodwill. Everything could carry on as usual, so long as no international embarrassments arose.

Then around the mid-nineties a new and perceptible force kicked in called "Globalization"; a virulent cancerous form of power control which in effect wrestled democratic processes away from ordinary folks at the ballot box in favour of the big multinational corporations, banks and most significantly the ginormous international bodies such as the E.U. and O.E.C.D. and the like.

In the former scenario those entities lobby and bribe to get the laws that suit their financial ambitions and in the latter the elected politicians have let their powers be subsumed to power crazed unelected bureaucrats that run those organizations. This isn't whacko conspiratorial stuff. I fully recollect one FCO high official here, in a rare moment of candor, saying how they were forced to enact these garbage worthy rules and legislation in the Islands. No kidding. Now we are hamstrung with them. Ironical isn't it that we saw the demise of the Soviet Bloc only to recreate it for ourselves in the West.

There is a wonderful acronym which could apply to the Islands, K.I.S.S. (Keep. It. Simple. Stupid.). Complicated matters simply do not sit well here and it's part of the Islands charm. The amount of reporting and data gathering that goes on now also represents unneeded stress to every day living. It's largely a waste of time and represents pure power play by bureaucrats trying to justify their existence. As the old adage goes "give people of mediocre ability too much power and they simply get drunk on it."

The general idea is that we all live in a global gold fishbowl where privacy counts for nothing (of course that doesn't necessarily apply to them) and we are all recorded as data rather like cattle being ear ticketed. Great isn't it! Everything seems to be depersonalized and we are addressed in incomprehensible jargon.

In the private sector, take banking for instance. Try following up with a query to your bank, usually following a message that something utterly irritating has been done "for your convenience". Usually it is to save them money at your expense and inconvenience.

You get on a telephone, where some fatuous mechanical voice tells you that this message is being recorded for quality control i.e. you are going to be recorded on a data base, so your details can be sold to advertisers who mysteriously contact and pester you out of nowhere.

Then you might get outsourced, usually to India or Mexico (resulting in some poor soul whose has worked for the bank for years, with a mortgage and family to support, to lose his job, just so the bank can save money) where after an eternity you get some guy sounding as if he is operating from a desk alongside a motorway, who after an age cannot bring up your details. "Try again later, is there anything else I can help you with." You need a second mortgage to pay the telephone bill for the phone you have just hurled at the wall out of exasperation.

What is truly scary about all this is that people are turning into troglodytes. All they want to do is stare at iPhones, even when walking along (they must be a muggers delight). Ironical isn't it how communication is the profitable theme nowadays and yet there is less actual communication between people at all. It is significant that the likes of Einstein, Orwell and Hawking all have predicted that mankind's downfall will be overreliance upon technology. If you subscribe to the evolutionary Darwin theory, in future children will probably evolve being born with iPhones as natural appendages to the rest of their physical form.

Reverting to the big controlling organization theme, it is easy to see how 'Orwell's' 1984 and Margaret Attwood's 'A Handmaid's Tale' could actually come about! These aren't just daft imaginative folks spinning a story. People don't question things anymore and the democratic process as we know it has been subverted seriously.

Not so long ago I was questioning the sense in some E.U. or O.E.C.D. directive, which they just rubber stamp in the Islands without question. I was talking to some officious sounding individual, querying the incomprehensible waffle that was being summarily enforced upon us, who simply said "It must be right it came from the E.U.". Rather like Moses coming down from the Mount with his stone tablets of the Commandments. Gawd help us all! They just swallow this stuff hook, line and sinker. It brought to mind another innovative expression created during these times we live in. I really had no idea what a friend of mine was talking about when the description "Jobsworth" came up in conversation. Literally it means 'more than my job is worth to do otherwise'. Then it clicked, pertaining to bureaucrats who rate rules and regulations way above basic common sense. Yep, there is no shortage of them nowadays; the world is full of them, often imbued with power way beyond their abilities. They think, but do not know how to think! Intoxicated with the power that it is unwisely bestowed upon them.

Although change is inevitable there seems a marked contrast between the generations of today and yesteryear; particularly many of the characters outlined in this book. Today's attitude embodies a sense of entitlement and everything is predicated around money and mercenary pursuits. There are exceptions of course. But the sort of characters in this book grew up having experienced the Second World War; the most terrifying event in recollected history perhaps and those people who experienced it felt lucky just to come out of it alive. It tended to generate a sort of altruism between one another which today is lacking. It may sound corny but it is true. Our ancestors, many of whom participated in the Second World War, would I suspect be turning in their graves to see what has become of the freedoms they fought for. Today's world is a ruddy mess thanks to poor leadership, mindless bureaucracy and greed.

Chapter 30

Wrexit and Lemon Aid

Two things happened over the past couple of years and which were surprising and also serve to up date the time line of this story. They both impacted the Islands through the U.K. and functioned as a wake up call so to speak.

Firstly, the Brexit vote in 2016 underscored how the UK politicians and civil servants had surreptitiously surrendered the U.K. laws and sovereignty to Brussels and Strasbourg down the years; rather like Goya's Saturn devouring its children. A true lemming leap over the cliff if you like. The whole thing is a complete mess, whereby it deems one size fits all; look at the disparity between Germany and the fate that has befallen Greece. Not forgetting the vast immigration and unemployment problems that exist in Europe.

The Euro has proven a disaster (although thankfully the U.K. resisted going into that, albeit that the likes of Messrs. Major and Blair were begging to get into it). It is a Utopian dream that has spawned disaster; it's open border policies and meddling in the Middle East have created wars and a migratory problem throughout Europe that will persist for decades. It is very much a case of the road to hell being paved with good intentions. Idealism at its worst. As the Romans maintained "If you want peace then prepare for war".

Brexit probably will not last, despite the fact that a majority in the U.K. voted for it. Those in power, especially powerful moguls, heads of Government are avidly against it and will do their damndest to frustrate it, despite what the majority want. That is the new world order (already alluded to) that serves itself and of course "knows best" (actually it's more lucrative for them, which is usually what this is all about). We sometimes suffer these experts in the Islands, which explains this diatribe.

Keep this in mind also, the Europeans are both vengeful and united in their opposition to the U.K. for daring to want to get out. The latter being absolutely disparate and all over the place in their negotiating positions. They are weak bargainers. Their leader, the Prime Minister Theresa May, wasn't even in favour of Brexit and prevaricates. When fighting a war you don't put in your frontline troops you captured from the other side and whose heart isn't in the fight.

What really rankles is that the powers in the E.U. and O.E.C.D. making these decisions which so profoundly affect our lives are unelected bureaucrats, idealistic academics (living in a parochial bubble) or failed wannabe politicians, often with little or no practical experience of anything. They are masters at being profligate with expense accounts; their snouts firmly immersed in the publicly funded trough or awarding themselves gold plated pensions and perks. Comically they excel at priding themselves as gourmets (or should I say gourmands) wallowing like hippos in their Michelin starred restaurants. It's nice work if you can get it.

Their behaviour can be boorish as well; often pontificating arrogantly. It reminds me of that wonderful expression Disraeli had of Gladstone "he is inebriated with the exuberance of his own verbosity". Come to think of it the inebriated part is pretty apt as well! They are possessed of a sort of short sighted cunning, which whilst extricating them from one set of problems only serves to land them in the vexations of the next. They are the sort of blokes who, if they were playing blind man's bluff in a harem, they would probably end up with the eunuch!

Mind you the E.U. works just dandy for the big corporations and banks, who lobby and bribe the E.U. for the laws they want. For small businesses it is a poisoned chalice. As a German wine grower put it, "Why can't I just be let to get on tending my vines, instead of filling out one hundred pages of regulatory answers." You get the drift. We are dealing with power crazed bullies here, meting it out to the little guy. Could you see the U.S. for one moment accept being bullied by a bunch of bureaucratic Muppets based in Brussels!

They are control freaks and there is little justification for their meddling in the affairs of the Islands. This is a U.S. theatre of influence and not European. Even that fairground barker to the North, sporting a dead red squirrel on his head doesn't pester us this way. But if we voted out on Brexit why are the E.U. still dictating terms to us. The vote was in or out, not out but only if or subject to this and that! It is the Establishment usurping the rights of the Electorate and democracy becomes a shambles.

Of course this sort of ranting is prone to get you ranked as a pariah to the pro E.U. Remainer Brigade and these remarks are about as popular as a pork pie in a synagogue to them (actually we need some Jewish pragmatism to address these problems). Why is it so many are anti the British identity and its heritage. Did you realize there are even some official and twisted nerds who want to demolish Nelson's Column in Trafalgar Square. It's one of the statutory trust bodies!

There are even efforts to obliterate British history in schools there now. Forget political correctness, facts are facts, whether palatable or not sometimes. Orwell again probably coined this with perspicuity when he said "England is perhaps the only great country whose intellectuals are ashamed of their own nationality". It certainly resonates.

The second event which struck me as being as momentous and even ludicrous was Hurricane Irma in 2017. We actually had two devastating category five hurricanes a few weeks apart. Please will someone strangle these idiots who claim climate change isn't a reality. The destruction and misery defy description and the hellish aftermath will endure for a long time.

Now the likes of Messrs. Cameron and Blair who, like all politicians want to look good on the world stage, saw fit in the case of the former, to enshrine into law a vast sum of money to be put aside each year. This was something like thirteen billion pounds, to go towards countries in need and designated for good causes.

You might think the U.K. would administer their own monies. Not one bit of it. The handling is entrusted to that hideous confederate of the E.U., the O.E.C.D., bless their cotton socks, who deem that whilst the likes of North Korea are eligible for the aid, the Dependent Territories, including the Turks and Caicos Islands are considered too rich. This is a total falsehood as there is a good deal of poverty in the Islands and contrary to the O.E.C.D. belief they are not overrun with rich tax exiles. It's all part of their chip on the shoulder resentful attitude or perhaps just unadulterated ignorance.

This is also embarrassing, not that today's politicians and civil servants give one iota, because in two World Wars, the Islands, other Dependent Territories, and Commonwealth countries such as India, Canada, Australia and New Zealand to name but a few, unselfishly gave of their lives to help the U.K. stay afloat in its wars against the European powers. This was undoubtedly the case and crucial up until 1941, before the U.S.S.R. and U.S.A. entered the conflict, when the circumstances were diar. These politicians and bureaucrats are conveniently forgetful of history, which also has a nasty tendency of repeating itself. They have vacillating loyalties.

There is a tendency to develop a somewhat cynical view of politicians as time goes by. The pre-requisites for that role apparently being to have an ego the size of the Eiffel Tower, an ability to lie convincingly and charisma. There are some exceptions of course, but it's not the norm. Climbing that greasy totem pole of politics you have to be ruthless, taking scalps as you crawl your way to the top. As Mark Twain so eloquently put it: "Politicians and diapers must be changed often, and for the same reason".

There are agencies that have sprung up to administer that aid. Often by parties who have uncomfortably close connections with Government and who make a corrupt packet into the bargain. Governments such as India have asked us not to send it because it ends up in the wrong pockets; they even have their own space programme, so are scarcely on their uppers so to speak.

You have some bizarre purposes for which the aid is put to. For example curing flatulence in cows in Columbia or encouraging performers in Ethiopia to make a career out of juggling. Five million pounds was given to develop an Ethiopian version of the Spice Girls; not to relieve hunger which exists there mark you. No kidding. Meanwhile old age pensioners in the U.K are left to die on the floors of the A and E departments in the under funded hospitals there. And the politicians say they want to look good!

Have you also noticed how there is never any shortage of large consulting firms and experts around to secure lucrative contracts in carrying out assessments and reports into these problems. Often it is a journey into the bleedin obvious and addressing problems which they have been part of. Rendering no benefit in the outcome save for a large fee for themselves. The Islands get this all the time, although no one has the gumption to say anything. It's a well established racket.

It would be nice not to have to recount much of this stuff, but when all said and done it is an irrefutable part of life nowadays. Someone once gave a perfect description to all those shenanigans and ethical peoples efforts to counteract them. They likened it to a barrel of Florida crabs they had once seen. As soon as one makes the effort to get out for a better life and nearly reaches the top to escape the others haul him back to their level in the barrel.

It is true that the E.U. sometimes donates aid to the Islands and the like, but you have to look at it askance and be wary. We are not talking about some wealthy benign aunt here, doling out the old spondulicks to her nephews and nieces. Alas everything has a price and who pays the piper calls the tune. They always want to control countries that accept their offerings. It is very much the donkey, cart, carrot and stick scenario.

In real terms the E.U.'s policies towards Caribbean nations can be atrocious, particularly with regard to the tariffs they put in place for the goods these poorer nations seek to export. The E.U. is all about self aggrandizement; just look at their corrupt agricultural policies. These bureaucratic clowns even have a committee for examining the curvature of imported bananas! Simply job creation for themselves and prejudicial to Caribbean exporting nations. There is something rotten in the

State of Denmark and it ain't cheese!

Before the emergence of globalization countries were so much more interesting with their different boundaries, cultures and histories. Even travel was more civilized as opposed to half the population nowadays being miserably shunted around the world in cattle truck style transportation and spending hours in battery hen styled airports. It's as if someone has taken the Mona Lisa picture and wiped over it with a wet sponge, leaving an uninteresting amorphous blob. The colours have run. Someone once depicted various countries of the world within that sort of context, illustrating the contrast. At the top Sri Lanka, dark, verdant, exciting, secretive and alluring. Down to the other end of the scale, Siberia; everyone knows where it is but nobody wants to go there! The latter equating to the effects of globalization.

Surprisingly some globalizations I could buy into, like standardizing electrical sockets worldwide for appliances. How about the total elimination of typing. Aren't these devices that anticipate your words maddening. Or better still ridding ourselves of wires attached to electrical equipment; the time you spend trying to untangle them, or is it just me?

Why not, instead of leveling everyone and ruling every facet of our lives, do something practical and to everyone's enjoyment. It's human nature that there will always be some more equal than others. Mankind is by nature a contentious beast and greedy, unlike the animal kingdom we are so busy eliminating from this planet. Common sense and courtesy should be the order of the day and it makes life far more pleasurable. Try to preserve good things and not indulge in change for changes sake, simply because it makes money.

I better stop as this is rapidly assuming the boring characteristics of a sermon.

Epilogue

Okay, the last two chapters were a tad too serious. I suppose looking back we were spoiled and, you know, it's still one hell of a life to be had here. Just not quite what it was and in any case if I carry on like this I will be dismissed as a crank. Life is to be enjoyed and where better than in the Islands.

Having finished this drivel I am going to my favourite resort. Order a long drink and watch the sunset. After all these years I still haven't seen the famous green flash, that occasionally occurs when the yellow sun dips beneath the blue sea. I have seen pictures of it and who knows I might get lucky this time.

Even if that doesn't happen I will be planning our trip to North and Middle Caicos for the weekend, to get away from the hustle and bustle of Provo life, where life is still as it used to be. I started with Treasure Island , so I might even meet another self imposed eccentric castaway, getting away from it all, or a Baloo the Bear type studying relaxation; a test pilot for hammocks. I probably will never meet the sort of characters I have described, but it's still a great place to hang out.

In any case it's the perfect setting to nurture ideas for another book. As the thoroughly entertaining late journalist and raconteur Christopher Hitchens said, "everyone has a book hidden inside them" and then typically went on to add "and in most cases that's where it should stay". Help!

At odds with the world? Not one bit of it. Nor trying to emulate the pioneer backwoodsman Daniel Boone, who having lived in splendid isolation for years in a cabin in the mountains, one day saw a puff of smoke about ten miles away on the horizon and resolved to move on as the place was 'getting crowded'! Nope, simply busy finding lots of things not to do and enjoying the place. Try it sometime. There's nothing quite like controlling your own time.

LARRY LARKING

Biography

Larry Larking is a Brit transplant from the UK to the Turks and Caicos Islands. A Robinson Crusoe happily beachcoming the shores of life, keenly interested in history and curious places. They always wanted to send their best to the Islands, but he wasn't avaliable, so they sent him. Now a permanent and contented inhabitant of the Islands, with little inclination to go anywhere else. Life as a beach bumpkin has much to commend. Why not?"

CPSIA information can be obtained
at www.ICGtesting.com
Printed in the USA
JSHW071021010223
37138JS00005B/10